MAKING TOYS FOR INFANTS AND TODDLERS

Using Ordinary Stuff for Extraordinary Play

Linda G. Miller

Mary Jo Gibbs

Illustrated by Kathy Dobbs

Dedication

From Mary Jo Gibbs

My personal thanks

To my children Kevin, Kim, and Kelly for providing me with my first and best experiences with children

To my grandchildren Tylon, Hunter, Logan, Kayleigh, Kelsey, Drew, Ansley, and Kyle, who think my ideas and activities are "so cool"

Special thanks to my husband Joe, who truly believes I can do anything and supports my efforts 100%

To Linda Miller—"My best friends bring out the best in me." Thanks, Linda

From Linda Miller

For creative teachers everywhere, and to those who (like me) like to see some directions. Happy teaching!

From Kathy Dobbs

For my husband Dale and son Sam—I love you both!

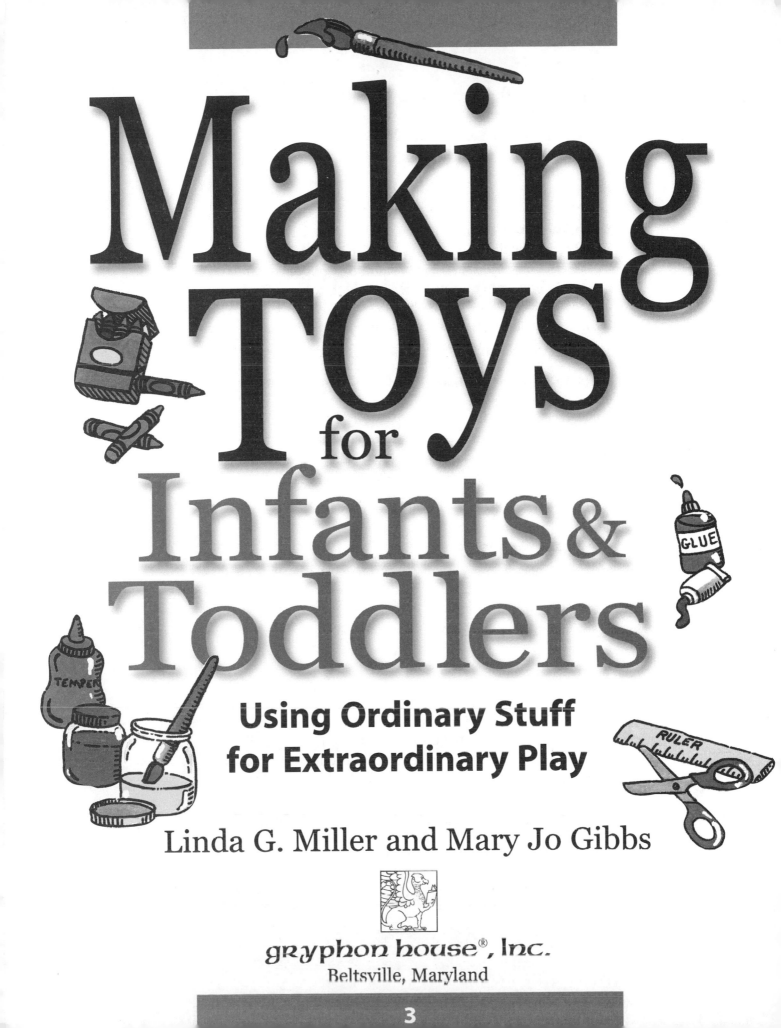

Making Toys for Infants & Toddlers

Using Ordinary Stuff for Extraordinary Play

Linda G. Miller and Mary Jo Gibbs

gryphon house®, Inc.
Beltsville, Maryland

Copyright

©2002 Linda G. Miller and Mary Jo Gibbs
Published by Gryphon House, Inc.
10726 Tucker Street, Beltsville, MD 20705
301.595.9500; 301.595.0051 (fax); 800.638.0928

Visit us on the web at www.gryphonhouse.com

Illustrated by Kathy Dobbs

Library of Congress-Cataloging-in-Publication Data

Miller, Linda G.
  Making toys for infants and toddlers : using ordinary stuff for extraordinary play / Linda G. Miller, Mary Jo Gibbs ; illustrated by Kathy Dobbs.
       p. cm.
Includes index.
  ISBN 0-87659-249-3
  1. Educational toys. 2. Educational games. 3. Early childhood education--Activity programs. I. Gibbs, Mary Jo, 1946- II. Dobbs, Kathy. III. Title.
  LB1029.T6 M53 2002
  371.33'7--dc21

                                                        2002007412

Bulk purchase

Gryphon House books are available at special discount when purchased in bulk. Special editions or book excerpts also can be created to specification. For details, contact the Director of Sales at the address or phone number on this page.

Disclaimer

The publisher and the authors cannot be held responsible for injury, mishap, or damages incurred during the use of or because of the activities in this book. The authors recommend appropriate and reasonable supervision at all times based on the age and capability of each child.

Table of Contents

Introduction

Teachers of young children are some of the most creative individuals around; however, from time to time everyone needs fresh ideas. The experiences presented in this book are simple and inexpensive, allowing teachers to focus on quality interactions with the children in their care. To determine which activities are appropriate for the children in your care, first observe to see where they are developmentally and what their needs and interests are. Record what you observe using anecdotal notes, so you will have a record of the children's progress.*

Parents often think that purchased toys are superior to found or created items. However, young children often prefer the box or even the wrapping paper to the purchased toy inside. Boxes are wonderful toys for stacking, carrying, nesting, filling, dumping, and matching. Children love climbing into and out of boxes, and very large boxes make great playhouses.

Boxes and other simple materials are also inexpensive "raw materials" for creating high-quality learning toys for young children. Toys also can be made from gloves, mittens, socks, pantyhose, and bags. Always begin with items that are completely empty and clean. The key to using found and discarded items as toys is being open to the limitless opportunities and the imagination of a child. Think of the difference between a child playing with a toy phone that is always a phone and a box that can be a house, car, truck, train, step, and so on. It is the open-ended nature of these toys that makes them better than many purchased toys and a great way for young children to learn.

Making Toys and Finding Materials

(Adapted from *Innovations: The Comprehensive Infant and Toddler Curriculum* by Kay Albrecht and Linda G. Miller)

Making toys and finding interesting materials for young children to manipulate and play with do not need to be expensive or difficult tasks.

* You can find a blank anecdotal note form in *Innovations: The Comprehensive Infant Curriculum* on page 428 and in *Innovations: The Comprehensive Toddler Curriculum* on page 470.

Teachers often find that everyday discarded household materials and teacher-made toys are by far the most interesting to children. And, this approach accommodates an important consideration for infants and toddlers—the novelty of new things.

Using teacher-made toys allows teachers to use the same idea in a different way to interest children in activities and materials. For example, empty plastic soft drink bottles can be used in many ways. Filled with water and interesting small objects that glitter and swirl when shaken, they make a good toy for a non-mobile infant to look at while lying on a quilt on the floor. With a short piece of twine attached to the neck, the bottle can be pulled along as a crawler moves around the room. Lined up like bowling pins, the soft drink containers make perfect targets for new walkers to push over with their hands and feet as they walk forward.

Consider the following guidelines for teacher-made toys for infants and toddlers:

- Make sure the toys encourage action and/or interaction, rather than passive watching.
- If possible, make the toys responsive. If it is not possible for the toy to be responsive, plan to use it with a responsive adult close by.
- Make multiple toys. Infants and most toddlers cannot wait for a turn, so don't ask them to do so.
- Try to make toys that are multi-sensory with a variety of uses. That way you'll get more out of the ones you do make.
- Check each homemade toy for safety. Then check it again, and ask another teacher to check it. Be sure that you do not overlook safety issues in teacher-made toys. Get some help in insuring that the toys are safe. Before making the toy, begin with safe, clean recycled materials. Periodically recheck the toys for safety.

Common household objects that are safe for children (even if the child decides to see how it tastes) are sometimes great toys. Ideas for toys that can be made from common objects include:

- **Shaker Bottles**—Put small, colored pieces of dry cereal or other objects inside any clear plastic bottle. Empty, clean plastic shampoo or dishwashing detergent bottles make great toys for young children. Glue and tape the lids on tight.
- **Simple Hand Puppets**—Puppets, made from socks for example, are a good way for an adult to talk with an infant or toddler and to capture a young child's attention.
- **Boxes**—All shapes and sizes of boxes are appropriate for walking around or crawling into, sitting in, stacking, nesting, putting things in, and dumping them out. A shoebox with a short length of twine attached makes a good pull toy for a crawler.

- **Sorting Toys**—A cardboard egg carton or a cupcake tin works well as a place in which to put objects (for example, large spools, blocks, cereal). It is important that the objects are large enough not to be swallowed. Be sure to test each object with a choke tube.

- **Dress-Ups**—Infants and toddlers enjoy putting on hats and carrying purses, especially if there is a mirror (unbreakable), so that they can see themselves.

- **Blocks**—Use milk cartons of different sizes (half-pint, quart, half-gallon) to create blocks. Each block requires two cartons. Cut off the tops and put one bottom inside the other, so the bottoms of the cartons make the ends of the block. Put a small object such as a bell inside some blocks, so that they will make a noise when shaken. Tape securely and cover with self-adhesive paper.

- **Texture Blocks and Scraps**—Cover blocks of wood (approximately 5" x 3" x ¾" and sanded to prevent splinters) with brightly colored fabric of different textures (such as burlap, corduroy, velvet, quilted material, voile, and net).

- **A Cup of Dry Cereal**—How many things can an infant or toddler do with a cup of dry cereal? A LOT! (Yes, one of the first things he or she will do is dump the cereal on the floor!)

- **Books**—Use books even with very young babies. They like to look at the shapes and colors, and they enjoy having teachers point out objects in the books and turn the pages to see what's next. A relatively "child-proof" book can be made by cutting large, bright, interesting pictures from magazines, pasting them on construction paper, covering both sides with clear self-adhesive paper, and putting the pages in a loose-leaf notebook. Old wallpaper sample books are great for infants and toddlers to use by themselves to practice page-turning skills.

- **Hanging Toys**—Many common household items, such as paper cups, large spools, and aluminum foil pie plates, can be attached to a piece of string or yarn and hung for a very young baby to look at. When babies begin reaching (around 4 to 5 months), suspend objects so the baby can try to reach them while lying on the floor or sitting in an infant seat. Clips to attach things from the ceiling are available at hardware stores. Bars to suspend objects can be made easily from plastic pipe. Hanging toys/objects must be securely attached to short lengths of elastic, string, or yarn. Closely supervise children playing with toys/objects that are suspended. Things that hang over cribs should be removed when a baby can grasp the toy or object.

- **Containers**—Plastic or metal (be sure edges are smooth) containers of all sizes and shapes can be used for stacking, nesting, putting objects in, and dumping things out.

- **Sorting Can**—Cut the plastic lid of a coffee can so only certain shapes and sizes (blocks, spoons, for example) will fit through.

- **Hidden Objects**—With the child watching, put something into a paper bag or box or under a diaper. See if he or she will try to find it.

The beauty of teacher-made toys is that they are novel and interesting without costing much money and can be discarded when they get worn out. New toys can be made to replace used ones, keeping the environment interesting and fun. Create lots of teacher-made toys for infants and toddlers in each developmental area. Teacher-made toys keep the job of planning fresh and give both the teacher and children ways to create play together.

Experiences for Infants and Toddlers

(Adapted from *Innovations: The Comprehensive Infant and Toddler Curriculum* by Kay Albrecht and Linda G. Miller)

This book does not use the traditional idea of interest areas. After all, many infants are not yet mobile—much less walking. It is the teacher's responsibility to bring the activity to the infant or carry the infant to the activity. Toddlers are much more likely to follow the lead of other toddlers instead of choosing individual experiences on their own.

New situations are interesting to infants and toddlers, especially when they are in a secure environment where they feel confident to try new things. Teachers often interact both with the child and with the new toy or situation (called triangulation). In this way, the infant or toddler finds interest in the novelty, while feeling the security of having a familiar adult near.

Additionally, teachers must look to children to determine how to proceed in the classroom. Observe the child first to determine what activity or experience is the right one and to determine if the child is receptive. If appropriate, do the activity with the child. Observe again to determine if you need to continue. Record your observations. Experiences are situations that seem to occur naturally in the course of the day, while activities are planned events for children. The teacher may plan an activity involving a stroller ride around the playground. The children experience the sights, sounds, and joy of being outside.

Activities in this book are included in the following categories:

Dramatic Play—Beyond durable and washable dolls that represent a variety of ethnicities, infants and toddlers need props such as the ones they see in the real world, especially things associated with Mom or Dad (for example, purses, hats, bracelets, toy key rings, and so on). The teacher's role includes supplying play cues, participating with children as they play, and labeling what infants and toddlers do as they take on different roles. Dramatic play experiences contribute to children's vocabulary development and to their comprehension of the real world.

Literacy—Provide access to sturdy, inexpensive, replaceable books including cloth books, board books, and plastic books. Display them to the right or the left of the child's shoulders to stimulate gazing and focusing skills.

Give children the opportunity to experiment with and learn about books on their own, actively interacting with them. For infants, this may simply mean mouthing and chewing on books. These early experiences with books as sources of interesting images and stimulation form the foundation of literacy.

Read to children every day. Make reading books a priority with infants and toddlers, one at a time or in pairs and trios. Additional literacy opportunities exist with rhymes and fingerplays. The rhyme and repetition in language are important for literacy development. Include many opportunities during the day to involve young children in this kind of interaction.

Gross Motor—Infants and toddlers always need a clean, padded area where they can be placed to stretch, wiggle, turn over, push up, and rest. A gym mat with a washable cover works well. Padded stools or hassocks are excellent for babies to use to pull to a stand and to cruise along the edges. The teacher's role is interactive. Particularly with emerging skills, teachers should help infants and toddlers practice skills, yet be near enough to provide support and prevent serious spills and tumbles.

Fine Motor—Young children actively explore their environments through their senses. Many of their experiences are tactile in nature. As young children grow and mature, their fine motor skills develop. Experiences included under fine motor are ones that will allow children to explore using the small muscles of their hands.

Sensory and Art—Sensory and water experiences are a mainstay of infant and toddler programs. Water is soothing. Water toys stimulate play, and the splashing and slapping of water produce interesting reactions. Art activities for young children are really sensory in nature. Very young children (unlike adults) don't care about the end result of an art activity. Instead, they are experiencing the moment—enjoying the feel of the fingerpaint, the smell of the crayons, and the texture of the paper. Be sure to date all projects and note each child's name who participated.

Curiosity—Young children are curious about the world in which they live. They want to find out what is in it and how everything works. They enjoy exploring new things in the environment. For example, for infants, discovering the properties of an assortment of rattles is a delightful means of interacting with them. One type of curiosity or problem-solving experience for young children includes opportunities for reaching and grasping. This fosters independent play and a variety of motor skills such as pulling, batting, and swinging arms and legs. Another type of problem solving for young children involves experimenting with interesting materials, both old favorites and new ones. These include easy manipulatives, small square blocks, and plastic jars with tops to undo. The role of the teacher is to interact with the children and provide plenty of invitations to play.

To spark the curiosity of infants and toddlers place unbreakable mirrors placed at children's eye level. A child can catch a view of a teacher who may be busy with another child, discover him or herself, look at other children, and observe the surrounding environment. Teachers at Reggio Emilia consider the child's own image as one of the most interesting images children explore during the first three years (Edwards, Forman, and Gandini, 1998).

Outdoors—Outdoor time is an important part of the day for very young children. The fresh air is a nice change from the closed environment of the classroom. Additionally, activities that are moved from the inside to the outside take on a new meaning. The sounds of the neighborhood, the way light changes because of clouds or shade, and the feel of the breeze all add to the richness of the outdoor experience. Outdoor experiences also provide a change of pace and variety for the teacher. Outdoors, the teacher's role is interactive, inviting children to learn as they explore.

How to Use This Book

The book is divided into seven sections:

- Dramatic Play
- Literacy
- Gross Motor
- Fine Motor
- Sensory and Art
- Curiosity
- Outdoors

Within each section, activities are organized by:

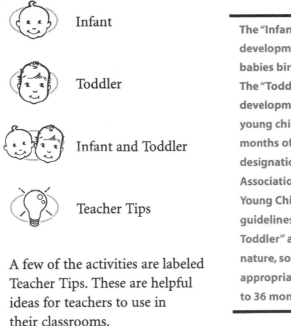

Infant

Toddler

Infant and Toddler

Teacher Tips

The "Infant" activities are developmentally appropriate for babies birth to 18 months of age. The "Toddler" activities are developmentally appropriate for young children 18 months to 36 months of age. These age designations match National Association for the Education of Young Children (NAEYC) guidelines. The "Infant and Toddler" activities are broad in nature, so these activities are appropriate for children newborn to 36 months of age.

A few of the activities are labeled Teacher Tips. These are helpful ideas for teachers to use in their classrooms.

Activities are also organized by material used:

Bags

Boxes

Gloves/Mittens

Socks/Pantyhose

These materials are inexpensive and easy to find. Bags include paper lunch bags, grocery bags, zipper-closure bags, and plastic bags. Boxes include cardboard boxes, shoeboxes, take-out food containers, cereal boxes, milk cartons, and potato chip canisters.

Teachers may choose to use this book in many ways.

- Teachers can scan activities and choose according to what materials they may have available.
- Teachers may choose activities based solely on developmental level from each of the main sections.
- Teachers may use the book for ideas to provide a well-rounded, developmentally appropriate classroom for young children by selecting activities from each of the seven sections throughout the book. Ideas in each section provide choices of activities within each age range.
- Teachers may also use the book to get fresh ideas for a theme-based curriculum. Activities are included that are appropriate for a wide variety of themes.

Interpreting Each Activity

Each activity includes the following:
- Materials
- To Make
- To Use

Materials—Includes all essential materials needed to complete the activity. Materials are generally arts and crafts supplies that are familiar and easily accessible to teachers. Every effort has been made to use materials that are free, recycled, or very inexpensive. Always keep in mind safety precautions when using any materials, and especially if you substitute materials other than those listed. Closely supervise children, so they do not put dangerous items (such as bags) into their mouths.

To Make—Explains how to create the activity. This section provides step-by-step instructions for creating the toy. Many activities are illustrated to make the process even easier. It is always advisable to try the activity before presenting it to a child or involving a child in the activity. Think about safety and be aware of tools or materials used by an adult that are not intended for small children. Often, teachers will be directed to use certain tools away from the children.

To Use—Suggests ways to use the activity with a child or children; however, teachers and children may very well find their own ways to enjoy the activities. Follow all safety precautions, and supervise children closely at all times.

Dramatic Play

Hand Puppets

 Infants

Gloves/Mittens

Materials

baby mittens or socks

colored non-toxic permanent markers or needle and thread (adults only)

To Make

- Draw or sew faces on the mittens or socks.
- Or, if desired, add full body details including clothes.

To Use

- Put the socks or mittens on an infant's hands.
- Narrate the child's actions as she moves and notices her hands with the puppets on them.

Foot Puppets

 Infants

Socks/Pantyhose

Materials

baby socks

colored non-toxic permanent markers (adults only)

To Make

- Draw faces on baby socks and place them on the infant's feet. Use bright colored markers to add interest.

To Use

- Place the socks on an infant's feet.
- Comment on the foot puppets as the infant moves her feet.

Stuffed Bag Pumpkin/Apples

 Toddlers

Bags

Materials
paper lunch bags
newspapers
tape or yarn
orange, green, or red paint
paintbrushes
black markers

To Make
- Stuff lunch bags with crumpled newspapers and secure the opening with tape or yarn.
- Help the children paint the bags to look like apples or pumpkins.
- Use markers to make details.

To Use
- Place apples or pumpkins in dramatic play.
- Talk with the toddlers about the colors they chose and about the objects as they play.

Tall Bag Hats

 Toddlers

Bags

Materials
small- or medium-size paper grocery bags
art materials

To Make

- Fold down the opening of the bag until it fits a child's head.
- Use paint, crayons, markers, glue, and other art materials to decorate the hat.

Hint: Decorate the hats to relate to a theme or a child's interest. For example, draw a fire truck on it if the child likes fire trucks.

To Use

- Toddlers wear the tall hats as they play.

Paper Bag Hats

Toddlers

Bags

Materials

large, brown paper bags
scissors (adults only)
laminate or clear contact paper, optional

To Make

- Cut off the bottom of the bag, and then cut the bag on the seam side so that it lays flat.
- Fold the bag to make a sailor hat.
- Or cut out a large circle (about 18"), and then cut out a circle (about 4") from the center of the larger circle to make a floppy hat.

Hint: Hats last longer if they are laminated. Laminate flattened bags first (or cover them with clear contact paper), and then make hats.

To Use

- Toddlers wear the hats as they play.

Box Creatures

Toddlers

Boxes

Materials

different sizes of cardboard boxes (tissue, cereal, food)
duct tape
paint
paintbrushes
art supplies

To Make

- Tape three or four different-size boxes together end-to-end.
- Working with the children, use paint and art supplies to create unique creatures.

To Use

- Use in dramatic play or place the creatures on the playground to enrich outdoor play.

Flower Box

 Toddlers

Boxes

Materials
construction paper, in a variety of colors
scissors (adults only)
tape
craft sticks
small shoebox
sand

To Make
- Cut out flower shapes from colored construction paper.
- Tape the flower shapes onto craft sticks.
- Fill the shoebox with sand.
- "Plant" the flowers in the sand.

To Use
- Toddlers will enjoy planting the flowers and then taking them out again.

Doll Bed

 Toddlers

 Boxes

Materials
shoebox with lid
scissors (adults only)
paint and paintbrush, or contact paper
fabric scrap

To Make

- Cut the lid of the shoebox in half horizontally.
- Discard one half of the lid.
- Glue the saved half to the inside of one end of the shoebox to make a headboard.
- Paint or cover the doll bed with contact paper.
- Cut the fabric into a rectangle and place it inside for a blanket.

To Use

- Place the doll bed in dramatic play for children to use with the dolls.

Telephone Booth

Toddlers

Boxes

Materials

craft knife (adults only)
large appliance box
markers
toy telephone

To Make

- Away from the children, use a craft knife to cut two windows and a door into the box.
- Use a marker to write the word "telephone" on the sides of the box.
- Place a toy phone inside the box.

To Use

- Interact with toddlers as they play in the telephone booth.
- Extend their comments by adding to what they say or restate what they say in a complete sentence to make this a literacy experience.

Car Wash

 Toddlers

Boxes

Materials

large appliance box
craft knife (adults only)
garbage bags
tape
markers

To Make

- Away from the children, use a craft knife to cut out a large tunnel from two sides of the box.
- Cut the garbage bags into narrow strips.
- Tape the strips to the inside of the tunnel, so they hang down in the "entrance" and "exit."
- Use markers to write "Entrance" and "Exit" over the openings.

To Use

- Toddlers ride tricycles or "scoot toys" through the car wash.

Sizing Socks

 Toddlers

Socks/Pantyhose

Materials
different sizes of socks
basket or cloth bag for storage

To Make
■ Place a variety of socks in the basket or bag.

To Use
■ Toddlers find socks the same size. They may need help putting on the socks. As they play with the socks, they will take them off (they will learn to do this first) and put them back on.

Paper Bag Stick Puppets

 Infants/Toddlers

Bags

Materials
paper lunch bags
newspapers
paint stir sticks
tape
construction paper
scissors (adults only)
glue
short lengths of yarn
fabric strips

To Make

- Stuff each bag with crumpled newspapers.
- Place a stir stick about halfway into each bag. Tape the opening securely closed.
- Cut out facial features from construction paper. Make a face on each bag by gluing the construction paper facial features onto the bag.
- Glue on short lengths of yarn for hair and make construction paper hats, collars, or shirts. Use fabric strips for clothing.

To Use

- Use these puppets to present poems, fingerplays, and books to the children. Also, use them during routine times throughout the day.

Grocery Bag Turkey

 Infants/Toddlers

 Bags

Materials
large brown paper grocery bag
newspapers
rubber band
paper lunch bag
tape
scissors
construction paper
glue

To Make

- Stuff the large paper bag with crumpled newspapers until full. Use a rubber band to close the bag.
- Fill the smaller lunch bag with crumpled newspapers and shape it into a "head."
- Attach the head onto the bag body using tape.
- Cut out eyes, a beak, a wattle, and feet from appropriate colored construction paper.
- Tape or glue the construction paper features onto the bags.
- Cut out a variety of colored construction paper feathers and attach for wings and a tail.

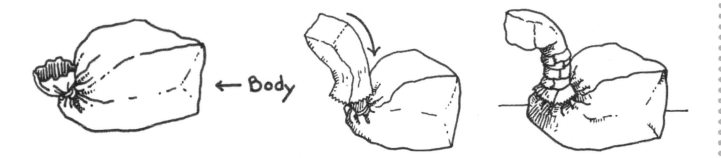

← Body

To Use

- Place the turkey in dramatic play for children to enjoy.

Cardboard Food Box Blocks

Infants/Toddlers

Boxes

Materials
different sizes of cardboard food boxes
newspapers
masking tape

To Make
- Stuff the boxes with newspaper and tape the openings closed.

To Use
- Children use the boxes to build in the block area.
- Or, they may carry the blocks around or use them in dramatic play.

Post Office Mailbox

Infants/Toddlers

Boxes

Materials
cardboard box
craft knife (adults only)
red, white, and blue paint
paintbrushes
paper and pencils
junk mail
envelopes

To Make

- Away from the children, use a craft knife to cut a slot into one side of the box.
- Paint the box red, white, and blue to look like the post office mailboxes.

To Use

- Children can "write" their own letters and seal them in envelopes to mail or use junk mail to put into the slot.

Bear Cave

Infants/Toddlers

Boxes

Materials

large cardboard box
craft knife (adults only)
tape
paint, optional

To Make

- Away from the children, create a bear cave by cutting an archway into a large cardboard box. Remove any staples.
- Reinforce the archway and box with tape, and cover or smooth the edges.
- You may want to use the "cave" inside for a while, and then rekindle interest by letting the children paint it outside.

To Use

- Place the bear cave in dramatic play.
- Put stuffed bears in the cave, so children can hug and snuggle them.
- Read books about bears and other animals that live in caves.

Bucket Space Helmets

 Infants/Toddlers

 Boxes

Materials

craft knife (adults only)
fast-food chicken buckets
paper cups
glue
non-toxic silver spray paint (adults only)

To Make

- Away from the children, use a craft knife to cut out a rectangular hole in the side of the bucket.
- Glue paper cups on the sides and on the top of the bucket.
- Away from the children, spray paint the bucket and cups with non-toxic silver paint.
- Make a number of helmets because very young children are not able to share.

To Use
- Children wear the helmets as they play.

Stuffed Glove

Infants/Toddlers

Gloves/Mittens

Materials
cotton gloves
fibcrfill
needle and thread (adults only)
non-toxic permanent markers (adults only)

To Make
- Stuff the glove with fiberfill.
- Sew the opening securely closed.
- Use permanent markers to draw facial features on the palm of the glove.

To Use
- The glove makes an excellent washable doll, puppet, or throwing toy.

34

Literacy

- Read to children every day.
- Post a list of the books you read to children. Place a date by the book title each time you read the book to show the importance of repetition.
- Do not expect all young children in your group to sit still while you read. Instead, read to two or three children at a time and allow children to move away as their interest changes.

Baby's Photo Album

 Infants

Bags

Materials

cardboard
scissors (adults only)
resealable plastic bags
photos of baby and baby's family
glue
hole punch
yarn

To Make

- Cut cardboard to fit inside the plastic bags.
- Glue photos on the pieces of cardboard.
- Put each photo into a plastic bag.
- Use a single-hole punch to punch two holes into the left sides of the bags (the "unzipped" side). Thread yarn through the holes and tie in a knot.

To Use

- Show the pictures to a baby, saying the appropriate names as you point to the pictures.
- Use the "Baby's Photo Album" throughout the day to help the baby connect with family members.
- Add to the album as new events occur and as family members change.

Tube Pictures

 Infants

Boxes

Materials
craft knife (adults only)
oatmeal box
glue
photos and magazine pictures
clear contact paper

To Make
- Away from the children, use a craft knife to cut off the top and bottom of an oatmeal box.
- Glue photos or magazine pictures of familiar objects onto the remaining cylinder.
- Cover the cylinder with clear contact paper.

To Use
- As a baby rolls the cylinder, say the names of the pictured objects.

Finger Book

 Infants

Boxes

Materials
cardboard box
craft knife (adults only)
markers
hole punch
yarn

To Make

- Away from the children, use a craft knife to cut a cardboard box into 8" squares.
- Draw pictures on the squares with markers.
- Away from the children, use a craft knife to cut holes into the pictures that you or an infant can push fingers through. Suggestions include an elephant with a hole for the trunk, a dog with a hole for the tail, a bunny with two holes for ears, or a person with two holes for legs.
- Punch holes into the sides of the pages and fasten the pages together with short lengths of yarn.

To Use

- Show the book to a baby, using your fingers to make the pictures move.
- Watch his reaction to determine how to continue playing.
- After a while, encourage the baby to put his fingers into the holes to make the pictures wiggle.
- Talk and laugh as you play with him.

Hand Jive

 Infants

Gloves/Mittens

Materials
gloves

To Make
- Place a glove on your hand and wiggle your fingers.

To Use
- Recite nursery rhymes, songs, or fingerplays and move the glove accordingly.
- Place the glove on the baby's hand and observe what he does.
- Sing the following song.

I Like Gloves (Tune: "Are You Sleeping?")
I like gloves.
I like gloves.
How about you?
How about you?
I like to wiggle my fingers.
I like to wiggle my fingers.
How about you?
How about you?

Food Box Book

 Toddlers

Boxes

Materials
scissors (adults only)
food boxes
hole punch
yarn

To Make
- Cut off the fronts and backs of food boxes.
- Punch holes into the left side of the boxes. Fasten the pages together with yarn to make food books.

To Use
- Use the food books to talk with children about different foods.

Simple Sock Puppets

Toddlers

Socks/Pantyhose

Materials
socks
non-toxic permanent markers (adults only)

To Make
- Use permanent markers to draw faces on the socks.

To Use
- Children use their puppets as you recite the following rhyme.

Little Puppet
Little puppet, little puppet,
Go down and touch my toes.
Then come up
And land on my nose.

Little puppet, little puppet,
Go and find my knees.
Now find my shoulders
And pat them, please.

Little puppet, little puppet,
Fly over my head so high.
Now take time
To cover my eyes.

Lastly, little puppet friend,
I'll hold you on my chest.
It's time now
To take a little rest.

Animal Tails

Toddlers

Socks/Pantyhose

Materials

pantyhose
scissors (adults only)
fiberfill
non-toxic paint
paintbrush
yarn
tape

To Make

- Cut off the legs of a pair of pantyhose, about 12" long. Stuff the legs with fiberfill.
- Tie a secure knot in the opening.
- Use different colors of non-toxic paint to decorate a variety of animal "tails."
- When the paint is dry, tie a short piece of yarn to the knotted end of the tail to tie the tail onto toddlers' clothing.

To Use

- Tape a tail onto the toddler's clothing.
- Observe him to determine his reaction.
- If he shows continued interest, make animal sounds as he wears the tail.

Grocery Bag Books

 Infants/Toddlers

Bags

Materials

fast food restaurant bags
hole punch
yarn

To Make

- Collect a variety of familiar fast food restaurant bags.
- Punch holes into any edges of the bags and fasten them together with yarn to make a book.

To Use

- Provide grocery bag books as well as other teacher-made books throughout the classroom.

Grocery Bag Scribble Books

 Infants/Toddlers

Bags

Materials

large paper grocery bags
scissors (adults only)
hole punch
yarn
crayons

To Make

- Cut off the fronts and backs of grocery bags.
- Punch holes into the sides of the bags. Fasten the "pages" together with yarn.

To Use

- Give each child a scribble book.
- Children use crayons to scribble on the pages.
- Label each bag book with the child's name.
- Use this as a repeated experience.

Grocery Bag Big Books

 Infants/Toddlers

 Bags

Materials

large paper grocery bags
hole punch
silver book rings
storybook
markers
magazines and paste, optional

To Make

- Lay the grocery bags on their sides, with the bottom on the left and the opening on the right.
- Punch holes into the bottoms of the grocery bags on the left side.
- Fasten them together with silver book rings.
- Choose a storybook and rewrite it on the pages of the paper bag book.
- Draw or paste magazine pictures on the pages for illustrations.

To Use

- Big books are useful because they are a novelty for young children. They also make it possible for several children to see the book at once.

Baggie Books

Infants/Toddlers

Bags

Materials

construction paper
scissors (adults only)
zipper-closure plastic bags
photos or magazine pictures
glue
hole punch
ribbon

To Make

- Cut construction paper to fit inside the resealable bags.
- Glue photos or magazine pictures onto the construction paper pieces.
- Insert each picture into a resealable plastic bag and seal it.
- Put several of these together, punch holes in the sides, and fasten them together with short lengths of ribbon on the zippered side.

To Use

- Read print books and look at picture books with the children every day.

Note from the Authors

Baggie books are an inexpensive way to provide the large number of books needed in the classroom. Meet young children's need for novelty by adding books frequently.

Vehicle Books

Infants/Toddlers

Bags

Materials
poster board
scissors (adults only)
zipper-closure plastic bags
magazines, catalogs, or sales flyers
glue
markers
duct tape

To Make
- Cut poster board to fit inside the plastic bags.
- Cut out pictures of vehicles from magazines, catalogs, or sales flyers and glue them onto the poster board pieces.
- Label the pictures using lowercase print.
- Place the pictures into resealable plastic bags with the zippered side on the left.
- Use duct tape to attach the pages at the zippered side to form the book.

To Use
- Read the labels of the pictures as children look through the book.
- If they name the vehicles, expand and add to what they say.

Traffic Jam Books

Infants/Toddlers

Bags

Materials
pictures of cars, trucks, and trains
scissors (adults only)
poster board
zipper-closure plastic bags
glue or tape
marker
hole punch
yarn

To Make
- Cut out pictures of cars, trucks, and trains.
- Cut poster board to fit into the plastic bags.
- Glue or tape pictures to the pieces of poster board.
- Label each vehicle using lowercase print.
- Place each picture into its own resealable plastic bag.
- Punch holes both on the left side and the right side of each bag, and then thread short lengths of yarn through the holes.
- Tie the yarn to create an end-to-end traffic jam book.
- Use different sizes of plastic bags to create small and large books.

To Use
- Talk about the vehicles as you look at the book with the children.
- Add to the book as the children learn about different vehicles when you read other books.

Seed Books

Infants/Toddlers

Bags

Materials
cardboard
scissors (adults only)
large, zipper-closure plastic bags
glue
plants and/or seeds
hole punch
metal book rings or short lengths of yarn

To Make
- Cut cardboard to fit inside the plastic bags.
- Glue parts of plants and/or seeds onto the cardboard pieces.
- Place each piece of cardboard into its own resealable bag. Seal it closed.
- Punch holes into the left side of each page.
- Attach the pages together using metal book rings or short lengths of yarn.

To Use
- Point to objects in the book and name them.
- Add to the book as children experience new plants and seeds.
- Check the bags carefully for safety.

Lunch Bag Books

Infants/Toddlers

Bags

Materials
paper lunch bags
pictures of animals
glue, markers, and hole punch
short lengths of yarn

To Make

- Fold the bottoms of about four or five lunch bags over to one side.
- Glue an animal picture onto each bag, so that part of the picture is hidden underneath the flap.
- Use markers to label each picture.
- Punch holes into the open ends of the bags and secure the pages together with short lengths of yarn.

To Use

- Children guess what the animal is, then open the flap to see the whole picture.
- Talk about the children's guesses with them.

Hand Bunny

 Infants/Toddlers

 Bags

Materials

paper lunch bags
markers
construction paper
scissors (adults only)
glue
string

To Make

- Draw a bunny face on the upper part of a paper lunch bag.
- Cut out bunny ears from construction paper and glue the paper ears to the bag.
- Tie a short length of string around the bunny's neck so that the middle finger can be inserted into the head.
- Cut a hole into each side of the bag, right below the string, for a finger and thumb to stick out.

To Use

- Wiggle your fingers and thumb to make the puppet move.
- Use the puppet to introduce story time and to interact with infants and toddlers during routine times.
- Observe how a child reacts to any puppet before touching him with it.

Cereal Box Books

 Infants/Toddlers

 Boxes

Materials

cereal boxes
newspapers
glue
construction paper or colored craft paper
scissors (adults only)
markers
photos of child and family members
clear contact paper

To Make

- Stuff a cereal box with old newspapers and tape the opening securely closed.
- Cut construction paper or colored craft paper to fit around the box. Cover the box with the paper.
- Glue photos of the child and the child's family members onto all sides of the box.
- Label each picture with appropriate words.
- Cover the entire box with clear contact paper.

To Use

- As each child plays with his box, point to the photos and say the appropriate names.
- Encourage the child to say the names and point to the photos.

Note from the Authors

Because young children have strong emotional connections with family photographs, children may want to carry the box around even when not playing with it. Photos of family members help children make important emotional connections during the day. Photos may even be used as security items.

Playing Hands

 Infants/Toddlers

Gloves/Mittens

Materials

gloves or mittens

To Make and Use

- Place gloves or mittens on a child's hands.
- Observe the child's reaction.
- If he shows interest, sing the following song to the tune "Row, Row, Row Your Boat."
- Clap your hands at appropriate times.

Hands, Hands
Hands, hands, where are your hands?
Clap your hands right now.
Hands, hands, where are your hands?
Clap your hands right now.

- Continue as long as the child shows interest.

Oven Mitt Puppet

 Infants/Toddlers

 Gloves/Mittens

Materials
solid-colored oven mitt
non-toxic permanent markers (adults only)
yarn
needle and thread (adults only)

To Make
- Use permanent markers to draw facial features onto the oven mitt.
- Use a needle and thread to attach short lengths of yarn for hair.

To Use
- Use the puppet to sing songs or talk with babies or toddlers.
- If desired, use oven mitts in animal shapes.

Mitten Rabbit

  Infants/Toddlers

 Gloves/Mittens

Materials
white felt
scissors (adults only)
needle and thread (adults only)
mitten
black and pink felt or permanent markers (adults only)

To Make
- Cut out ears from white felt and sew them securely onto the back of the hand part of the mitten.
- Cut out eyes from black felt and a nose from pink felt and sew them securely onto the mitten.
- If desired, you may choose to draw the features with permanent markers instead of using felt.

To Use
- Use the puppet as you sing and interact with babies and toddlers.
- Always observe their reactions before continuing.
- Check the mitten rabbit often for safety.

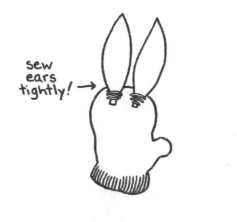

sew ears tightly! →

Sock Play

Infants/Toddlers

Socks/Pantyhose

Materials
socks

To Make and Use
- Put a sock on your hand and touch the child's toes.
- Encourage him to touch his toes as you sing the following song to the tune "Row, Row, Row Your Boat."
- This will be easier (and more fun) if the child is barefoot and seated on the floor.
- Brightly colored socks or socks with patterns will add interest.

Toes, Toes
Toes, toes, where are your toes?
Touch your toes right now.
Toes, toes, where are your toes?
Touch your toes right now.

Sock Dolls

Infants/Toddlers

Socks/Pantyhose

Materials
tube socks
fiberfill
non-toxic fabric paint or permanent markers (adult only)
yarn

To Make

- Stuff a tube sock with fiberfill.
- Tie a knot in the open end of the sock.
- Use fabric paint or permanent markers to draw a face on the sock doll.
- Create hair with permanent markers or sew on short lengths of yarn.

To Use

- Interact with children as they hug and carry their dolls.
- These dolls are washable.

Pantyhose Babies

Infants/Toddlers

Socks/Pantyhose

Materials

pantyhose
scissors (adults only)
fiberfill
non-toxic permanent marker (adults only)

To Make

- Cut off the legs of a pair of pantyhose, about 18" long.
- Tie a knot in one end of the pantyhose leg (if the foot portion is cut off).
- Stuff the hose with fiberfill and tie another knot to close the hose.
- Use permanent markers to draw facial features on the doll.
- Use a variety of colors of pantyhose to make multicultural dolls.
- If desired, sew short lengths of yarn to the doll's "head" for hair.

To Use

- Infants and toddlers will enjoy hugging, carrying, rocking, and talking to these cuddly dolls.

Note from the Authors

Encourage children to sing and talk to dolls. Also, use dolls as you read books to children.

Gross Motor

Stand and Push Box

 Infants

Boxes

Materials

sturdy cardboard boxes
file or sandpaper
colored contact paper or paint and brushes
stuffed toys

To Make

- Remove any staples and smooth all the rough edges of the sturdy box with a file or sandpaper.
- Paint the box or cover it with colored contact paper to add interest.
- Place stuffed toys inside the box.

To Use

- Observe as a baby sits or stands and explores the box. When she pulls up, she will be able to see the stuffed toys.
- When she is ready, show her how to hold onto the box and walk, pushing the box. She will walk independently when ready.

Drop and Fetch Toy

 Infants

Gloves/Mittens

Materials

glove
fiberfill
non-toxic permanent marker (adults only)
string

To Make

- Stuff the glove with fiberfill.
- Use a permanent marker to draw a face on the palm of the glove.
- Tie a short length of string around the opening of the glove and attach the other end of the string to a high chair.

To Use

- Babies drop the toy, and with some encouragement, can learn how to pull the toy back to drop it again and again. In this manner, they can play "drop and fetch" alone.

Kicking Glove

 Infants

Gloves/Mittens

Materials

jingle bells
glove
fiberfill
needle and thread (adults only)
blanket
low bar

To Make

- Put a jingle bell into each finger of a glove.
- Stuff the glove with fiberfill.
- Sew the opening securely closed.

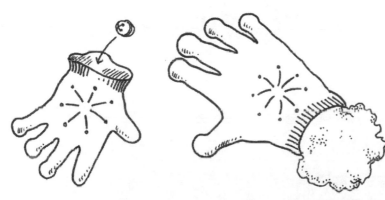 

To Use

- Place a baby on her back on a blanket on the floor.
- Hang the glove from a low bar, so the baby's feet can kick the glove.
- Show her how to kick the glove to make noise.
- Talk about what the baby is doing.

Pull and Stretch

Infants

Gloves/Mittens

Materials

pair of gloves
fiberfill
needle and thread (adults only)
elastic

To Make

- Stuff two gloves with fiberfill and sew the openings securely closed.
- Sew the ends of an 8" piece of elastic to each glove.

To Use

- Encourage a baby to hold one glove, while you hold the other one.
- Gently tug on the baby's glove to see how she will react.
- After playing "tug," gently pull on the glove and let go.
- Watch her reaction to the rebounding glove to know how to continue playing.

Wrist Bands

Infants

Socks/Pantyhose

Materials

children's socks in a variety of colors
scissors

To Make
- Cut off the cuffs of colored socks into narrow bands.
- Slip the bands onto baby's ankles and/or wrists.

To Use
- As the baby waves her arms about, the colorful bands attract her attention to her hands.

Caution: Use the wrist bands only while observing the baby. In a baby's mouth, wristbands may become a choke hazard.

Jingle Socks

 Infants

Socks/Pantyhose

Materials
baby socks
jingle bells
needle and thread (adults only)

To Make
- Sew jingle bells securely to the toes of socks.

To Use
- Place socks on the baby's feet.
- As she kicks her feet, the bells jingle.
- Describe what she is doing.
- Observe and record the reactions she has to the experience.

Caution: Examine the socks frequently to be sure the bells remain securely fastened to the sock.

Sock Hands

Infants

Socks/Pantyhose

Materials
baby socks
jingle bells
needle and thread (adults only)

To Make
- Turn a pair of baby socks inside out and securely sew jingle bells to the toe of each sock.
- Turn the socks right side out and place the socks onto the baby's hands.

To Use
- As the baby moves her hands, the bells will jingle and she will look for the noise.

Balancing Boxes

Toddlers

Boxes

Materials
small cardboard boxes (jewelry, crayon, food)
scrap paper or newspaper
tape

To Make
- Stuff small boxes with paper and tape them securely closed.

To Use
- Encourage toddlers to try to balance a small box on their head, hand, arm, or shoulder as they walk from one place to another.
- They may also wish to explore using the boxes in other ways (for example, carrying, lining up on the floor, stacking, and so on).

Putting on Gloves/Mittens

 Toddlers

Gloves/Mittens

Materials
large gloves or mittens

To Make and Use

■ Encourage the child to take off a glove or mitten as you sing the first stanza of the following song to the tune "The Mulberry Bush."

Putting on Gloves/Mittens
This is the way we take off a glove (mitten),
Take off a glove (mitten), take off a glove (mitten).
This is the way we take off a glove (mitten),
So early in the morning.

This is the way we put on a glove (mitten),
Put on a glove (mitten), put on a glove (mitten).
This is the way we put on a glove (mitten),
So early in the morning.

■ Later when the child is ready, use the song to encourage her to put on a glove or mitten.

Putting on Socks

Toddlers

Socks/Pantyhose

Materials
socks

To Make and To Use

■ Encourage one child to take off and put on a sock as you sing the following song to the tune "The Mulberry Bush."

Putting on Socks
This is the way we put on a sock,
Put on a sock, put on a sock.
This is the way we put on a sock,
So early in the morning.

■ Young children learn to take off socks and other types of clothing before they learn to put them on.

Sock Matching

Toddlers

Socks/Pantyhose

Materials
pairs of colored and patterned socks
basket

To Make
■ Mix socks together in a basket.

To Use
■ Children sort the socks to find matching pairs.
■ Name the colors of the socks as children play.
■ Some children will enjoy simply moving the socks from one place to another.

Weighing Socks

Toddlers

Socks/Pantyhose

Materials

tightly woven socks

variety of materials, such as dry rice, beans, marbles, cotton balls, or
shredded paper

To Make

- Fill tightly woven socks with different amounts of materials such
  as dry rice, beans, cotton balls, or shredded paper.
- Tie a knot in the opening of each sock. For added safety, place
  the full sock inside another sock and tie a knot in it, too.

To Use

- Toddlers pick up, carry around, and feel the weight of the sock.
- Narrate and describe what toddlers are doing, using terms such
  as *heavy* and *light*.
- Talk with the children about what is inside each sock.

Giant Pantyhose Balls

Toddlers

Socks/Pantyhose

Materials

pantyhose

scissors (adults only)

fiberfill

needle and thread (adults only)

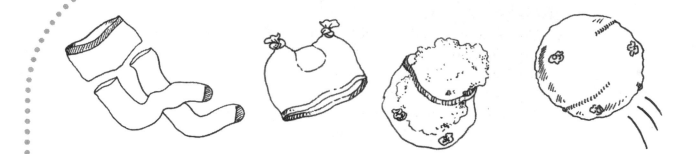

To Make

- Cut off the legs of three pairs of pantyhose. Save the legs for making other projects.
- Turn the panty portion of each pair inside out and knot the leg openings securely closed.
- Turn the panty portions right side out.
- Stuff one panty portion with fiberfill.
- Use a needle and thread to sew the opening securely closed.
- Cover the pantyhose ball with the next panty portion and sew closed.
- Repeat using the last panty portion.

To Use

- Toddlers use this large, soft pantyhose ball for beginning "catching" activities and inside or outside ball games.

Lunch Bag Blocks

 Infants/Toddlers

 Bags

Materials

non-toxic permanent markers (adults only)
paper lunch bags
newspapers
tape
marker

To Make

- Use permanent markers to draw houses, vehicles, and people on paper lunch bags.
- Stuff the bags with crumpled newspapers.
- Tape the openings securely closed.
- Create a print-rich environment by writing a label below each picture on the bag. Also, create blocks for children's names.

To Use

- Infants and toddlers use the bag blocks for carrying, dropping, pushing around, and building.

Open/Close Curtain

Infants/Toddlers

Boxes

Materials
medium size box
tape
cloth
toys

To Make

- Tape a piece of cloth over the opening of a box to make a "curtain."
- Throughout the week, put different toys inside the box.

To Use

- Observe children as they peek behind the curtain to see what is inside the box.

Swinging Door

 Infants/Toddlers

 Boxes

Materials
large cardboard box
craft knife (adults only)
duct tape

To Make
- Away from the children, cut off one continuous piece of one full side and a half side from the box.
- Use duct tape to attach the half side to a sturdy piece of furniture to create a swinging door going into dramatic play.

To Use
- Talk about "in" and "out" as the children play.

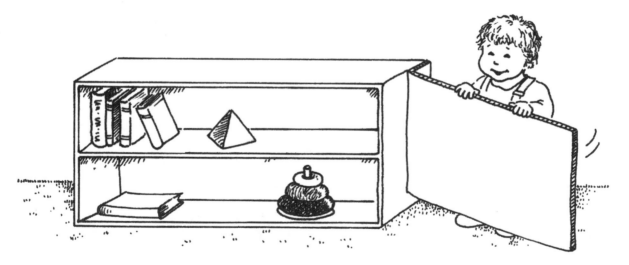

Crawl-Over Box

 Infants/Toddlers

Boxes

Materials
sturdy cardboard box
newspapers
tape
colorful contact paper
scissors (adults only)

To Make
- Tightly stuff the box with crumpled newspapers.
- Tape the box shut.
- Cover the entire box with colorful contact paper.

To Use
- Place the box on the floor for children to crawl over, push along the floor, or sit on.

Box and Lid Match

 Infants/Toddlers

Boxes

Materials
small and medium boxes with lids
paint
shallow trays
sponges

To Make

- Remove any staples and smooth all rough edges on the boxes and lids.
- Paint the boxes with the children. Since this is a very messy activity, it's a good idea to paint outside.
- Pour paint into shallow trays and paint the boxes using sponges.
- Supervise closely, so the children don't place sponges in their mouths.

To Use

- Talk about "on" and "off" as the children play with the boxes, putting on the lids and taking them off.

Milk Carton Blocks

 Infants/Toddlers

 Boxes

Materials

quart-size milk cartons
craft knife (adults only)
art materials
paint
paintbrush
liquid soap, optional
clear contact paper
tennis ball

To Make

- Away from the children, use a craft knife to cut off the tops of the cartons, leaving straight sides.
- Place one carton inside another.
- Encourage the children to use art materials and paint to decorate the cartons.

Tip: Adding a few drops of liquid soap to tempera paint will help the paint stick to the waxed carton.

- To make blocks last longer, cover them with clear contact paper.
- Place a tennis ball inside a few of the blocks for added interest.

To Use

- Add variety to the children's block play with these blocks.
- Talk with the children and describe the colors as they build.

Beanbag Mittens

 Infants/Toddlers

 Gloves/Mittens

Materials

small, zipper-closure plastic bags
dry beans (adults only)
mittens
short lengths of yarn

To Make

- Pour dry beans into small resealable bags and seal them closed.
- Place one bag inside each mitten.
- Tie the ends of the mittens closed using a short length of yarn.

To Use

- Children carry, drop, and throw these unusual beanbags.
- Inspect the mittens often for holes.
- To launder, cut off yarn and remove the plastic bags.

Ladybug Mobile

Infants/Toddlers

Gloves/Mittens

Materials

black gloves
fiberfill
needle and thread (adults only)
non-toxic permanent markers (adults only)
red felt
scissors (adults only)
elastic

To Make

- Stuff gloves with fiberfill and sew the openings securely closed.
- Cut red felt into circles that fit onto the backs of the gloves.
- Draw wings and black dots on the red felt to make ladybugs.
- Use a needle and thread to sew the ladybugs onto the backs of the gloves, allowing the stuffed fingers to hang down for legs.
- Sew a length of elastic to each ladybug and securely attach the other end of the elastic to the ceiling over the changing table or over an adult-size rocking chair.

To Use

- At the changing table, swing the ladybugs to get a child's attention.
- Encourage the children to reach for the bouncing ladybugs.
- Remove fiberfill and use them as puppets.

stitch red felt
ladybug securely...

Fine Motor

One-Piece Puzzles

 Infants

Boxes

Materials

cardboard boxes
craft knife (adults only)
colored paper
scissors (adults only)
glue
clear contact paper
elastic
tape

To Make

- Cut off the sides of a cardboard box (for cardboard pieces).
- Create a one-piece puzzle for infants. Glue a piece of colored paper to a piece of cardboard.
- Cover with clear contact paper.
- Away from the children, use a craft knife to cut out a simple shape from the center.
- Tape a piece of elastic to the puzzle piece to make a hand-pull for infants to grab and remove the puzzle piece.

To Use

- Observe the way each infant moves the puzzle piece. Notice how each child tries (or doesn't) to replace the puzzle piece.
- Record your observations.

Hand-y Sock

Infants

Socks/Pantyhose

Materials
baby sock
scissors (adults only)

To Make
- Cut five small holes in the toe section of a baby sock.

To Use
- Place the sock on the baby's hand with his fingers sticking out of the holes.
- As the baby wiggles his hand, the sock becomes an entertaining puppet.
- As he wiggles his fingers, wiggle yours, too.
- Talk about what you are doing.

Crinkle Snake

Infants

Socks/Pantyhose

Materials
pantyhose
scissors (adults only)
shredded paper
non-toxic permanent markers (adults only)

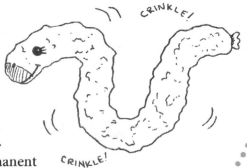

To Make
- Cut off the legs from a pair of pantyhose.
- Stuff each leg with shredded "noisy" paper.
- Draw features on the pantyhose with permanent markers.
- Tie a knot in the end.

To Use

- Give the "snake" to an infant to squeeze and make noises.
- Observe his reaction to determine how (or whether or not) to continue.

Advertising Signs

Toddlers

Bags

Materials

fast-food restaurant bags
scissors (adults only)
poster board
glue
tape
paint mixing sticks
clay

To Make

- Cut out logos from the fast-food bags and glue them onto poster board squares.
- Tape the signs to paint mixing sticks, and anchor the signs in a large ball of clay.
- You can also fold the squares so they can stand alone, or tape the signs directly to blocks.

To Use

- Signs can be used with blocks, in dramatic play, or as road signs for riding toys.

Drop Box

Toddlers

Boxes

Materials
oatmeal box
craft knife (adults only)
jar and juice can lids

To Make
■ Away from the children, use a craft knife to cut a slot into the
top of an oatmeal box. Make sure the slot is large enough for the
plastic jar lids to fit through easily.

To Use
■ Toddlers drop the lids in the slot.
■ Remove the box lid, so a toddler can dump out the jar lids.

Chalk Box

Toddlers

Boxes

Materials
socks
fiberfill
large sidewalk chalk
large cardboard box

To Make
■ Stuff a sock with fiberfill or other clean socks and tie a secure
knot in the opening.

To Use

- Help toddlers use chalk (supervise closely) to scribble on a cardboard box.
- Show them how to use the stuffed sock to erase the chalk to make a clean surface for drawing again.

Personal Felt Board Box

Toddlers

Boxes

Materials

cigar box, or any box with hinged lid
felt
glue
variety of colors of felt scraps
scissors (adults only)

To Make

- Cover the inside of the box lid with felt. Glue it in place.
- Cut out geometric shapes or figures from the colored felt scraps.
- Store the shapes inside the box.

To Use

- Toddlers sort, make designs, create patterns, or make up stories with the felt pieces.
- Observe children carefully to be certain they do not put the felt pieces into their mouths.

Cereal Box Puzzles

 Toddlers

 Boxes

Materials

cereal boxes
scissors (adults only)
markers
color dots
zipper-closure plastic bags

To Make

- Cut off the fronts of several cereal boxes.
- Use a marker to draw a simple puzzle design (2-3 pieces) on the back (plain side) of the cereal box covers.
- Cut out the pieces.
- Color-code the puzzles by putting a color dot on the backs of each piece, using a different color for each puzzle. If you don't have color dots, use a different color marker for each puzzle.
- Place each puzzle into a resealable plastic bag. Label each bag (for example, "crunch puzzle").

discard

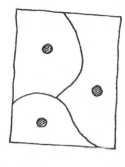

store in plastic bags!

To Use

- Make puzzles appropriate for the age and stage of the toddlers.
- Support children's learning by scaffolding—assisting children with tasks they can complete if the teacher helps their efforts.

Fast Food Boxes and Bags

 Infants/Toddlers

 Bags and Boxes

Materials

empty, clean fast food boxes and bags

To Make

- Young children love to play with familiar objects.
- Provide the children with clean boxes and bags with logos.

Note: Be sure the boxes and bags are safe for infants and toddlers to handle and "mouth."

To Use

- Children play "fill and dump" with various materials.
- This activity works well both inside and outside. You will be amazed at how many logos children will recognize and "read."
- Provide other props, such as a cash register, to support "fast food" play.

Tube Box

 Infants/Toddlers

Boxes

Materials
aluminum foil box
contact paper
non-toxic permanent markers (adults only)
scissors (adults only)
paper towel tube

To Make
- Remove the metal cutting edge on the foil box.
- Cover the inside and outside of the foil box with contact paper. To add visual interest, create a pattern using a permanent marker in a contrasting color.
- Cover the paper towel tube with another color or design of contact paper.

To Use
- Children place the tube in and out of the foil box, or just explore the tube.
- Add small unbreakable mirrors for interest.
- If children are beginning to talk, repeat their word(s) and add to them to make a complete sentence.

Building Portraits

 Infants/Toddlers

 Boxes

Materials

half-pint wax milk cartons, 2 per child
craft knife (adults only)
old newspapers
tape
photos of children
glue
marker

To Make

- Away from the children, use a craft knife to cut off the tops of the milk cartons.
- Place crumpled newspaper inside one of the cartons.
- Turn the other carton upside down and fit it inside the stuffed carton.
- Secure the cartons together with tape.
- Glue photos of the children on each of the six sides. Make enough carton blocks to put each child's picture on a block. If possible, make enough blocks so each child can have his own. Print each child's name below his picture.

secure with tape →

To Use

- Children build with these blocks. You also can use them to support name recognition.

Noisy Ball

 Infants/Toddlers

Socks/Pantyhose

Materials
cellophane paper (adults only)
old sock

To Make
- Crumple cellophane paper into a ball shape and push it into the toe of a sock. A colored or patterned sock will add variation and interest.
- Tie a knot in the end of the sock.

To Use
- When a baby or toddler squeezes the ball, the paper will make noise. Observe his reaction to determine what to do next.

Sensory and Art

Gardening Glove Texture Toy

 Infants

Gloves/Mittens

Materials
textured, cloth gardening gloves
fiberfill
non-toxic permanent markers (adults only)

To Make
- Stuff textured, cloth gardening gloves with fiberfill and tie a knot in the opening of each glove to close it.
- Use permanent markers to make colorful designs or draw facial features on the palm of the gloves.

To Use
- The textures on the fingers and palms of the gloves are interesting and different for babies to explore.

Texture Glove

 Infants

Gloves/Mittens

Materials
cotton gloves
textured fabric scraps
needle and thread (adults only)
large, textured buttons, optional

To Make

- Sew a different piece of textured fabric onto each fingertip of the glove.
- If desired, securely attach large textured buttons to some of the fingertips.

To Use

- Put the glove on your hand and encourage the baby to explore the different textures.
- Touch her hand with each of the textures as you talk about how the texture feels.

Caution: Make sure that the fabric scraps and buttons are secure on the glove and check them often to make sure they don't come loose.

Bags and Chalk Art

Toddlers

Bags

Materials

brown paper grocery bags
scissors (adults only)
large colored chalk
water, optional

To Make

- Cut large grocery bags into individual "papers" for each child.
- For a variation, soak the chalk in water before the children begin.

To Use

- Children draw on their brown paper with chalk. Using brown paper bags gives them a different texture experience.
- Repeat the activity often and label each picture with the child's name and the date.
- Display children's art by taping the papers together to form a banner.

Caution: Supervise closely to be certain that children do not put the chalk into their mouths. Discard chalk when it becomes small enough to pose a choking hazard.

Bags on the Easel

Toddlers

Bags

Materials
brown paper grocery bags
easel
paints
paint containers (for the easel)
variety of paintbrushes
scissors, optional
newspapers and tape, optional

To Make

- Clip a brown paper grocery bag onto the easel.
- Pour paint into containers used for the easel.
- Provide paintbrushes in a variety of sizes for toddlers to experiment with as they cover the bag with different colors of paint.

To Use

- Finished bags can be used in a variety of ways, such as:
  - costumes—cut out an opening for the head and armholes
  - giant bag blocks—stuff the bags with crumpled newspapers and tape them closed
  - wrapping paper

Sponge Print Pictures

Toddlers

Bags

Materials
scissors (adults only)
brown paper grocery bags
paint
aluminum pie tins
sponges
marker

To Make
- Cut off the wide sides of brown paper grocery bags.
- Pour paint into shallow pans.
- If desired, cut sponges into theme-related shapes.

To Use
- Children dip sponges into paint and make prints on the brown paper.
- Label and date all art experiences.

Caution: Supervise closely when using sponges, so children don't put them into their mouths.

Paper Bag Blocks

Toddlers

Bags

Materials
brown paper grocery bags
newspapers
tape
paint
shallow containers
paintbrushes
marker

To Make
- Fill grocery bags with crumpled newspapers, fold down the openings, and tape them closed.
- Pour paint into shallow containers.

To Use
- Encourage the toddlers to paint the bags.
- Label each bag with the child's name.
- When the bags are dry, the toddlers can carry, arrange, and stack the blocks.

Writing in the Snow

Toddlers

Bags

Materials
large zipper-closure plastic bags
¼ cup white paint
glue
duct tape

To Make
- Pour ¼ cup white paint into a zipper-closure plastic bag.
- Glue and tape the opening securely closed.

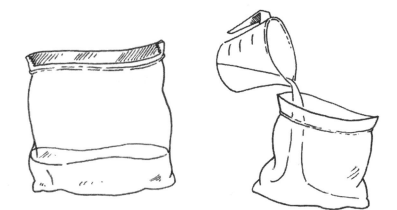

To Use
- The paint-filled bag will be easier to use if you tape it to a table or tray.
- Show toddlers how to press against the outside of the bag with a finger to form designs in the white paint.
- When finished with the design, toddlers can rub the bag to make the design disappear, and then start another design.

Sensory Bag

Toddlers

Bags

Materials
zipper-closure plastic freezer bags
non-toxic shaving cream or hair-setting gel (adults only)
glue
duct tape

To Make
- Fill a zipper-closure plastic bag with non-toxic shaving cream or hair gel.
- Seal the bag closed using glue and duct tape.

To Use

- Toddlers squeeze and squish the bags as a sensory experience.
- To vary the experience, try warming the bags in the sun or cooling them in the refrigerator.
- Talk with the toddlers as they have the different tactile experiences.

Caution: Supervise closely so that the children do not put the bags into their mouths.

Squish Bags

 Toddlers

Bags

Materials

smooth-textured, non-toxic, white or clear-colored products, such
   as shaving cream, whipping cream, and hair gel (adults only)
heavy-duty, zipper-closure plastic bags
food coloring (adults only)
duct tape
glue

To Make

- Place some of the white or clear-colored material into a zipper-closure plastic bag.
- Squirt a few drops of food coloring onto the material in the bag.
- Add more white or clear-colored material, so that the food coloring is surrounded by it.
- Glue and tape the bag closed.

To Use

- Show the children how to squeeze the bag to see the color changes.
- Talk with them as they observe what happens.

Caution: Supervise closely so that the children do not put the bags into their mouths.

Mixing Bags

Toddlers

Bags

Materials

cornstarch
sugar
water
measuring cups
pan
mixing spoon
hot plate or stove (adults only)
food coloring
zipper-closure plastic freezer bags
tape

To Make

■ Mix 1 cup (125 g) cornstarch, ⅓ cup (42 g) sugar, and 4 cups (960 ml) water in a pan.
■ Away from the children, cook over medium heat until thick.
■ Remove the mixture from the heat. Allow it to cool, and then separate it into thirds.
■ Make each third a separate color using red, blue, and yellow food coloring.
■ Put 1 tablespoon of each color mixture into plastic freezer bags, so that all three colors are in each bag.
■ Seal and tape the bags closed.

To Use

■ Children squeeze the bags and observe how the colors mix together to make new colors.
■ Narrate children's actions as they play.

Caution: Supervise closely so that the children do not put the bags into their mouths.

Spice Boxes

 Toddlers

Boxes

Materials

clean, empty spice boxes
small objects and materials, such as bells or dry beans (adults only)
glue
tape

To Make

- Provide clean, empty spice boxes for toddlers to play with.
- For variety, place small objects or materials inside the boxes (so the boxes will rattle).
- Glue and tape each box securely closed, being careful to leave the shaker holes on the top uncovered.

To Use

- Children explore stacking the spice boxes, smelling them, and shaking them.

Box Painting

 Toddlers

Boxes

Materials

paint
large pans
2" wide paintbrushes
cardboard boxes
old newspaper (if doing this activity indoors)

To Make

- Pour paint into pans large enough to accommodate the paintbrushes.

To Use

- Toddlers use large paintbrushes to paint the sides of the cardboard boxes.
- This activity can be very messy, so it is a great outdoor activity. However, you can do this activity indoors if you cover the floor with old newspapers.

'Round and 'Round Painting

Toddlers

Boxes

Materials

scissors (adults only)
paper
cylindrical boxes (oatmeal, potato chip canisters)
paint
Ping-Pong balls
marker

To Make

- Cut paper to fit inside the cylindrical box.
- Place the paper inside the box.
- Drop a few puddles of paint inside the box.
- Place two or three Ping-Pong balls in the box and securely close the lid.

To Use

- Toddlers shake the box, causing the balls to spread paint in unique designs on the paper.
- Remove the paper from the box.
- Talk about the different colors and shapes. Label all art creations with the child's name and date.

Box Rollers

Toddlers

Boxes

Materials

glue
textured materials, such as yarn, rope, sponge, fabric, and so on
round boxes
paint
shallow containers
paper
marker

To Make

- Glue textured materials on the outsides of round boxes. Let dry.
- Pour paint into shallow containers.

To Use

- Show the children how to roll the boxes in paint and then onto paper to make designs.
- Talk about the different textures.
- Label and date the designs.
- Display the paintings where children and parents can enjoy them.

Corrugated Paint Rollers

Toddlers

Boxes

Materials

craft knife (adults only)   cardboard box
tape   paint
shallow containers
paper

To Make

- Away from the children, use a craft knife to cut off the sides and flaps from a cardboard box.
- Remove the smooth paper from one side of the cardboard pieces, exposing the corrugated material.
- Make textured paint rollers by rolling the pieces into different sizes and lengths, leaving the corrugated sides facing out.
- Tape the ends securely into place.
- Pour paint into shallow containers.

To Use

- Show the children how to use the rollers by dipping them into paint and then rolling them on paper.
- These rollers make interesting textured designs. Talk about the designs as the children paint.

Box Collage

Toddlers

Boxes

Materials
large cardboard box
tape
contact paper
art materials
fishing line

To Make

- Tape the opening of the large cardboard box closed.
- Cover the sides of the box with contact paper with the sticky side out.

To Use

- Help toddlers stick art materials onto the sides of the box.
- Hang the box from the ceiling with a fishing line to display.

Yarn Gluing

Toddlers

Boxes

Materials

yarn
shoebox lids
glue
marker

To Make

- Help the children arrange pieces of yarn inside the shoebox lids to make designs.
- Once the yarn design is "arranged," dribble glue all over it.
- Allow the glue to dry.

To Use

- Hang the yarn creations on the wall. (They will look like paintings with frames.)
- Display at children's eye level.
- Label all art creations with the child's name and the date.

Table Easel

Toddlers

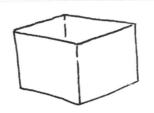

Boxes

Materials

large cardboard box
craft knife (adults only)
tape
glue or binder clips, optional
paint and paintbrushes
paper

To Make

- Away from the children, use a craft knife to cut off the top and bottom of a large cardboard box.
- Use the craft knife to cut one seam of the box, so that the four sides of the box lie flat (see illustration).
- Overlap two of the sides and tape them together.
- Fold over the other two sides of the box to make a triangle. Tape the sides securely in place.
- Glue, tape, or use binder clips to attach a pad of chart paper onto one side of the "easel."
- Place the easel on top of a table.
- If desired, turn the easel on its side and attach paper to all three sides. This allows more children to enjoy the art fun at the same time.

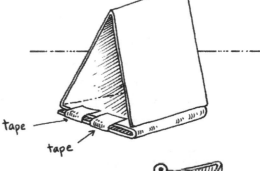

tape

tape

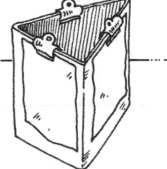

To Use

- Toddlers paint on the paper, and then they tear off the artwork and let it dry.
- The easel also works great outside.

Elephant Feel-y

 Toddlers

Boxes

Materials
cardboard box
craft knife (adults only)
gray paint
paintbrush
stapler
gray tube sock
duct tape
scissors (adults only)
felt
glue
variety of items for children to feel (see below)

To Make
- Away from the children, use a craft knife to cut out a hole on opposite sides of the cardboard box.
- Paint the box gray.
- Staple the open end of the tube sock around one of the holes in the box.
- Cover the staples with duct tape.
- Cut off the toe of the sock.
- Cut out eyes and ears from felt and glue them to the box.
- Choose items for children to feel such as blocks (wood, plastic, or cloth), dolls, toys, key rattles, large puzzle pieces, tennis balls, wallets, spoons, baby shoes, and so on. Place the items inside the box through the hole opposite the trunk.

To Use
- Children reach into the box through the elephant's "trunk" and guess what it is inside.

Glove/Mitten Painting

Toddlers

Gloves/Mittens

Materials
large paper
tape
fingerpaint
old gloves or mittens

To Make
- Tape a large piece of paper onto a tabletop.
- Drop puddles of fingerpaint on the paper.

To Use
- Help the toddlers put on gloves or mittens.
- The children use the gloves or mittens to smear the paint all over the paper.
- The gloves or mittens create a unique textured design and provide children with a different sensory experience. Some children may even make mitten prints!

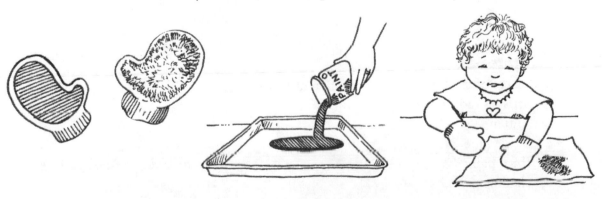

Glove Printing

 Toddlers

 Gloves/Mittens

Materials
scissors (adults only)
sponges
glue
gloves
paint
shallow containers
paper

To Make
- Cut sponges into a variety of shapes.
- Glue the sponge shapes onto the palms of the gloves. Let dry.
- Pour paint into shallow containers.

To Use
- Children put on the gloves, dip the sponges into paint, and make designs on the paper.

Hand Painters

 Toddlers

 Gloves/Mittens

Materials
pieces of cloth in a variety of different textures
scissors (adults only)
mittens
fabric glue
thick paint
shallow pans
paper
marker

To Make

- Cut the pieces of cloth to fit on the palm of each mitten.
- Glue a different texture to each mitten.
- Pour paint into shallow pans.

To Use

- Help the toddlers place mittens on their hands.
- They dip their textured mittens into paint and make prints and patterns on pieces of paper.
- Write the child's name and the date on each creation.

Big Ice Painting

Toddlers

Gloves/Mittens

Materials

plastic containers
water
freezer
empty, plastic salt shakers
dry tempera paint
butcher paper
mittens

To Make

- Fill plastic containers with water and freeze.
- Fill plastic salt shakers with different colors of dry tempera.
- Spread butcher paper on a table.

To Use

- When the ice is ready, help the children sprinkle dry paint onto the paper and then put on mittens.
- The children move the large ice shapes around the paper.
- As the ice melts, it mixes with the dry tempera to create colorful designs on the paper.

Caution: Discard ice pieces before they become small enough to be choke hazards.

Bubble-Wrap Mitts

 Toddlers

Gloves/Mittens

Materials

package bubble wrap
scissors (adults only)
duct tape
paint
shallow containers
paper

To Make

- Cut out pairs of mitten shapes from bubble wrap.
- Put the two matching shapes together and secure along the edges with duct tape, leaving the wrist side open.
- Show the toddler how to place her hand inside the "mitten."
- Pour paint into shallow containers.

To Use

- Place puddles of paint on a piece of paper. Show the toddler how to spread the paint using her bubble-wrap mitten.

Gadget Painting

Toddlers

Socks/Pantyhose

Materials

pantyhose
scissors (adults only)
large cookie cutters
thick tempera paint
shallow trays or paper plates
paper
marker

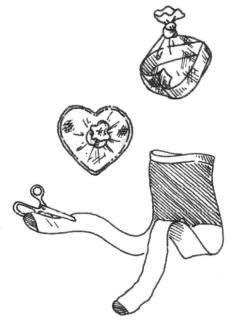

To Make

- Cut off the foot portions of pantyhose.
- Place a large cookie cutter into each cut-off foot section and tie a knot in the end.
- Pour paint into shallow trays or paper plates.

To Use

- Children dip the covered cookie cutters into the paint and press them onto pieces of paper.
- Talk about the texture prints created by the pantyhose.
- Label the prints with each child's name and the date.
- You can use this activity repeatedly. Change the color or type of paint and use the same paper.
- Label and date the prints each time the child repeats the activity.

Paint Daubers

Toddlers

Socks/Pantyhose

Materials

pantyhose

scissors (adults only)

paint

shallow containers

paper

fiberfill

yarn

To Make

- Cut off a 6" length of pantyhose.
- Cut along the length of the 6" pantyhose tube to make a rectangular piece of pantyhose.
- Place a small ball of fiberfill in the center of the rectangle.
- Pull up the edges of the pantyhose and secure them with a piece of yarn.
- Pour paint into shallow containers.

To Use

- Children dip the paint daubers into paint and then press them onto paper to make colorful designs.

Feel-y Can

Toddlers

Socks/Pantyhose

Materials

large tube sock

coffee can with a plastic lid

materials with a variety of textures,
    such as velvet or velour cloth,
    sandpaper, and a smooth ball

scissors (adults only)

contact paper or duct tape

To Make

- Cut off the toe of a large tube sock.
- Remove the lid from the coffee can. Stretch the cuff over the opening of the can.
- Tape the sock onto the coffee can using duct tape, or cover the entire can and the edge of the sock with contact paper.
- Place textured materials inside the can and put the lid in place.

To Use

- Toddlers put their hand inside the sock cuff and touch the textured materials inside the can.
- Talk with the toddlers about what they are feeling.

Caution: Make sure the textured materials pass the choke test before using them.

Portable Sensory Table

 Infants/Toddlers

 Boxes

Materials

shallow boxes (or medium-size boxes and scissors)
flour, soil, or sand
variety of small items, such as blocks, small toys, keys, dolls, and balls

To Make

- Collect shallow boxes or cut medium-size boxes in half.
- Fill the boxes with dry materials, such as flour, soil, or sand.

To Use

- Use the filled box as a sensory table inside or outside.
- Hide a variety of small items underneath the flour or soil for children to find.

Caution: Supervise closely, so children do not put the sensory materials into their mouths. Also, make sure that the small items pass the choke test.

Texture Box

Infants/Toddlers

Boxes

Materials

very large cardboard box, such as a refrigerator box
craft knife (adults only)
variety of textured materials, such as cloth (corduroy, velvet, cotton, denim, burlap, and silk), carpet, wallpaper, tree bark, sandpaper, and tape
glue

To Make

- Remove staples from the cardboard box and smooth any rough edges.
- Away from the children, use a craft knife to cut out a door and window. If you need better visibility of children, also remove the "roof."
- Glue a variety of textures to the inside and outside of the box.

To Use

- Infants and toddlers touch the textures with their hands and feet as they play inside and outside of the box.
- Talk about the different textures, colors, and shapes with the children.
- This Texture Box makes a great "getaway" for children who need time alone or time with a friend.

Texture Wall

 Infants/Toddlers

Boxes

Materials

large box
craft knife (adults only)
textured items, such as cloth and paper with different textures,
sandpaper, and so on
glue

To Make

- Away from the children, use a craft knife to cut off one panel of a very large box.
- Glue a variety of cloth, paper, and other items to the cardboard panel.

To Use

- Attach the panel to a wall at children's height.
- Children explore the textures on the panel.
- Talk about the different textures.

Caution: Test all items to be certain that they do not present a choke hazard.

Plastic Grocery Bag Smocks

Teacher Tip

Bags

Materials
plastic grocery bags with attached handles
scissors (adults only)

To Make
■ Cut off the bottoms of the plastic bags.

To Use
■ Children slip their arms through the handles to use the bags as disposable smocks.

Caution: Observe children carefully. Plastic bags can present a suffocation hazard.

Yarn Bags

Teacher Tip

Bags

Materials

balls of yarn
mesh produce bags
scissors

To Make

- Roll yarn into balls.
- Place several balls of yarn inside a mesh produce bag.
- Thread the ends of yarn through the holes to dangle from the bottom of the bag.

To Use

- Hang the bag at a convenient level.
- Pull out one strand of yarn and cut it.
- The yarn stays untangled, and the yarn balls are visible for choosing desired colors.

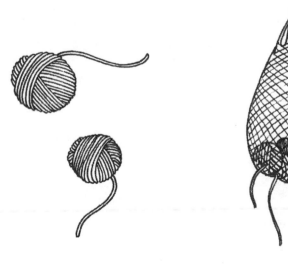

String Guard

Teacher Tip

Boxes

Materials

oatmeal container
contact paper
craft knife (adults only)
ball of yarn or string

To Make

- Cover the oatmeal container with contact paper.
- Away from the children, use a craft knife to make a hole in the lid.
- Drop a ball of yarn or string inside the container and thread the end through the hole in the lid.
- Replace the lid.

To Use

- Keep the container in a handy spot.
- Pull yarn or string through the hole and cut off the length as needed.

Curiosity

Windy Ribbons

 Infants

Bags

Materials
colored ribbons
mesh produce bag
pipe cleaners

To Make
- Tie colored ribbons through the holes of a mesh produce bag.
- Attach a pipe cleaner to one end of the bag and hang the bag on a tree limb or playground fence.

To Use
- Position the baby so he can watch the colorful ribbons flutter in the breeze.
- Be sure ribbons are out of reach of all children.

Rolling Photos

 Infants

Boxes

Materials
"noisy" materials, such as jingle bells, rice, beans, and so on
clean, empty potato chip canister
glue
tape
construction paper
photos
clear contact paper

To Make

- Place noise-producing materials, such as jingle bells, inside a potato chip canister.
- Glue and tape the lid securely in place.
- Cover the can with construction paper and glue or tape it in place. Then glue photos on the can.
- Cover the can and photos with clear contact paper.

To Use

- As the baby shakes and rolls the can, talk about the photos on the can.

Sea Bags

 Toddlers

Bags

Materials

small, zipper-closure plastic bags (freezer-ype)
sand
shells, colorful rocks, and sea animal shapes
glue
tape

To Make

- Pour sand inside the plastic bag. Add shells, rocks, and sea animal shapes. Use objects with smooth, rounded edges.
- Glue and tape the bags securely closed.
- Place the filled bag inside another bag. Glue and tape the second bag closed.

To Use

- Toddlers can examine the objects inside the plastic bags safely.

Caution: Observe children carefully to be certain that they do not put the bags into their mouths and that the bags stay securely closed.

Match Boxes

Toddlers

Boxes

Materials

scissors (adults only)
textured fabric
large matchboxes (sliding drawer type) or other slide boxes
glue

To Make

- Cut textured fabric to fit the inside of a matchbox.
- Glue the fabric inside the drawer.

To Use

- Children slide the drawers open to experience the textures.
- Talk about the textures and the terms *in* and *out* with the toddlers.
- With larger boxes, place toddler-safe toys or an unbreakable mirror inside the box. Observe toddlers' reactions.

Gift Box

Toddlers

Boxes

Materials

very large cardboard box
craft knife (adults only)
wrapping paper
scissors (adults only)
tape

To Make

- Away from the children, use a craft knife to cut off the top of a very large box.
- Wrap the box with colorful gift wrap.

To Use

- Toddlers love to climb into and out of boxes.
- When a toddler climbs into the box, ask, "Who is in the box?" Say the child's name and clap.

Bottle Box

Toddlers

Boxes

Materials

saltine cracker box
scissors (adults only)
contact paper
empty, plastic 2-liter bottle
"noisy" materials, such as dry beans, rice, rocks, and marbles
glue
tape

To Make

- Cut contact paper to fit around the cracker box. Cover the box with the contact paper.
- Fill the plastic bottle with a cupful of noise-producing materials.
- Glue and tape the lid securely onto the bottle.

To Use

- Toddlers put the bottle in and out of the box, making noise as they play "in and out."

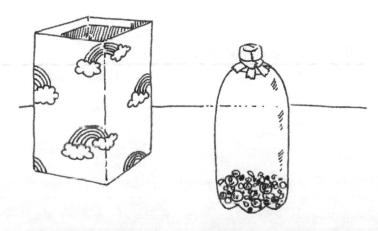

Magic Scarves

 Toddlers

Boxes

Materials

craft knife (adults only)
shoebox with lid or tissue box
colored scarves

To Make

- Away from the children, use a craft knife to cut out a round hole in one of the narrow ends of the shoebox.
- Tie the scarves together, end to end.
- Place the scarves inside the box with the end of the scarf just peeking out of the hole.
- Place the lid on the box.

To Use

- Toddlers pull the end of the scarf.
- Talk about the toddlers' actions and the colors of each scarf.

Shape Sorter Box

 Toddlers

Boxes

Materials
blocks in a variety of shapes
shoebox with lid
pencil
craft knife (adults only)

To Make
- Place a few blocks on top of the shoebox lid. Trace around the blocks using a pencil.
- Away from the children, use a craft knife to cut out the simple block shapes.
- Place the lid on the box.

To Use
- Toddlers match the blocks with their matching holes in the box lid.
- When all the blocks are inside the box, they can remove the lid and dump out the blocks to play again.

Talking Puppets

Toddlers

Boxes

Materials

clean, empty cardboard juice cartons
plain paper
scissors and craft knife (adults only)
glue
marker
art supplies

To Make

- Cut plain paper to fit around a juice box. Cover the juice box with the paper and glue it in place.
- Draw a line around the box, halfway between the top and the bottom.
- Cut along the line on the front and sides of the box, leaving the back of the box uncut.
- Fold the back of the box backward to loosen the "hinge." (The front is the part that is cut, and the back has the hinge.)
- Use art materials to make a face on the front of the box, making the box opening the mouth.
- Away from the children, use a craft knife to cut out two finger-size holes in the back of the box puppet (near the top) and one thumb-size hole near the bottom (see illustration).

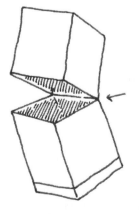 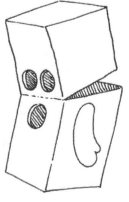 

To Use

- To make the puppet "talk," place two fingers through the top holes and a thumb through the bottom hole.
- Use the puppet to tell stories and fingerplays to the children, as well as for routine times.

Matching Mittens

Toddlers

Gloves/Mittens

Materials

distinct pairs of matching mittens
box or basket

To Make

- Place pairs of matching mittens into a box or basket

To Use

- Talk with the toddlers about *pairs, alike,* and *different.*
- Show them how to mix up the mittens and then match the pairs.

Magic Tube

Toddlers

Socks/Pantyhose

Materials

adult tube sock
scissors (adults only)
small toys that will fit into a sock

To Make

- Away from the children, cut off the toe portion of the sock to form a tube.

To Use

- Show the toddlers how to put toys into one end of the sock and then watch as the toys come out the other end.
- Talk about *in* and *out* as they continue to put toys into the tube sock.

Surprise Boxes

Infants/Toddlers

Boxes

Materials

photographs or unbreakable mirror
glue or tape
shoeboxes with lids

To Make

- Glue or tape photographs or unbreakable mirrors to the inside lids of shoeboxes.

To Use

- Children remove the lids of the shoeboxes. Observe them as they play and talk about what they see.
- Record your observations.

Bauble Box

 Infants/Toddlers

Boxes

Materials

clear, plastic take-out box with attached lid, such as a sandwich
  container
colorful materials, such as beads, craft gems, and glitter
glue
tape

To Make

- Place colorful materials inside the clear plastic container.
- Glue and tape the lid securely in place.

To Use

- Children shake the box and observe as the colors move around
  inside.

Rolling Noisy Box

 Infants/Toddlers

Boxes

Materials

"noisy" materials, such as bells, metal jar lids, and dried beans
oatmeal container with lid
tape
contact paper
scissors (adults only)

To Make

- Place noisy items inside the oatmeal container.
- Replace the lid and tape it securely in place.
- Cut contact paper to fit around the container. Cover it with
  contact paper.

To Use

■ Children shake, roll, or carry the noisy toy.

Tube Play

Infants/Toddlers

Boxes

Materials

empty, clean potato chip canisters
colored contact paper
scissors (adults only)
hole punch
elastic
"noisy" materials, such as bells, metal jar lids, and dried beans
glue

To Make

■ Cut colorful contact paper to fit around the potato chip canister. Cover the canister with the contact paper.

■ Away from the children, punch a hole into opposite sides of the canister near the top.

■ Tie a length of elastic through the holes and securely knot it in place.

■ Place noisy materials inside the potato chip can and glue the lid securely in place.

■ Use the elastic to hang the can from the ceiling over the diaper-changing table.

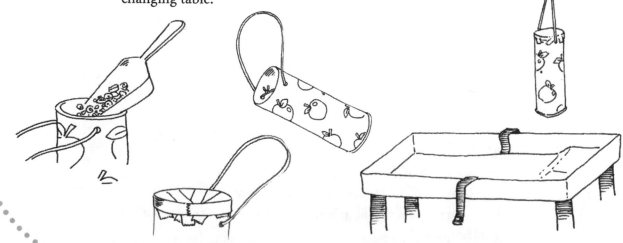

To Use

■ Swing the colorful tubes and encourage an infant or toddler to reach out and grasp the tube.

Caution: Carefully monitor this activity.

Glove Box

 Infants/Toddlers

 Gloves/Mittens

Materials

large shoebox with lid
craft knife (adults only)
variety of types of gloves

To Make

■ Away from the children, use a craft knife to cut out a large hole in the shoebox lid.

■ Place gloves inside the box. Some ideas for types of gloves to use include: dishwashing gloves, gardening gloves, heavy-duty work gloves, mittens, elbow-length evening gloves, leather and suede gloves, textured-palm gloves, golf or batting gloves, and a small child's baseball glove.

■ Put the lid on the box.

To Use

■ Children reach inside the hole in the box to touch and hold the different gloves.

■ Talk about how the gloves feel and what they look like after the children remove them from the box.

Mitten Streamers

 Infants/Toddlers

Gloves/Mittens

Materials

scissors (adults only)
colored ribbons
needle and thread (adults only)
old mittens
lively music

To Make

- Cut brightly colored ribbon into short lengths.
- Sew the ribbons onto the mitten securely.

To Use

- Play lively music and help the child place a mitten on his hand.
- As he moves the mitten, the ribbons will wave and flutter.
- This is also a good outdoor activity.

Stuffed Toy Puppets

 Infants/Toddlers

Gloves/Mittens

Materials

safe, stuffed toys
scissors (adults only)
mittens
needle and thread (adults only)

To Make

- Create puppets from stuffed toys. Rip the seam along the bottom of a toy.
- Remove some of the stuffing and insert a mitten.
- Sew the opening of the mitten to the ripped seam, so that the stuffing is completely contained.

To Use

- Use the puppets to encourage interactions with children.

Caution: Inspect the puppets regularly for safety.

Sock Garden

 Infants/Toddlers

Socks/Pantyhose

Materials

large tube socks
zipper-closure plastic bags
spray bottle
water

To Make

- Help toddlers and walking infants pull on a tube sock over their shoes and up their legs.
- Go outside and take a walk in tall grass.
- Carefully remove the socks and place each one into a resealable plastic bag.
- Use a spray bottle of water to wet the socks slightly.
- Seal the plastic bag and place it in a sunny window. In a few days, seeds will begin to sprout.

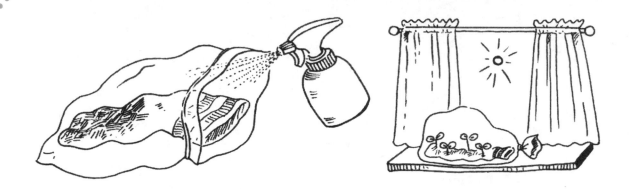

To Use

- Observe what is growing inside the bag each day and talk with the children about what is happening.

Outdoors

Cozy Box

 Infants

Boxes

Materials

pieces of cloth with different textures
glue
sturdy medium-size box

To Make

- Glue various pieces of cloth with different textures to the inside and outside of the box.

To Use

- Take the box outside.
- Infants will enjoy feeling the different textures as they pull up on the sides of the box.
- Sitting in small spaces such as the Cozy Box is an important way for infants to feel secure both inside and outside.

Holiday Collage Bags

 Toddlers

Bags

Materials

glue
grocery bags
collage materials, such as colored tissue, ribbons, and wrapping paper
sponge paintbrushes

To Make

- Bring the paper bags outside and lay them on the sidewalk.
- Spread glue on the bags.

To Use

- The children place collage materials on the glue.
- Show them how to pat down the materials using a sponge paintbrush.
- Allow the bags to dry completely.
- When the glue dries, the bags may be used for wrapping gifts, taking home artwork, or storing holiday decorations.

Note: This works great as an outside activity because it is so messy.

Big Blocks

Toddlers

Boxes

Materials

sturdy cardboard boxes with lids
newspapers
masking tape

To Make

- Stuff the sturdy boxes with newspapers.
- Tape the lids securely in place.
- Remove or tape over staples or rough edges.

To Use

- Children use the blocks to build large projects both inside and outside.

Tunnels

Toddlers

Boxes

Materials

cylinder-shaped boxes (oatmeal, salt, potato chip canisters)
craft knife (adults only)
duct tape
toy cars

To Make

- Away from the children, use a craft knife to remove the tops and bottoms of boxes.
- Place the cylinders end-to-end and use duct tape to connect them, forming a long tunnel.

To Use

- Bring the tunnels outside. Toddlers can roll toy cars through the tunnels.

Compartment Boxes

Toddlers

Boxes

Materials

craft knife (adults only)
cardboard box with individual compartments (such as those used to ship wine)
short piece of rope
empty plastic bottles, cardboard tubes, and toys

To Make

- Away from the children, use a craft knife to cut out a hole in the side of the box.
- Thread a rope through the hole and tie a knot in the end.

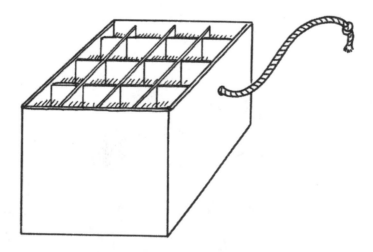

To Use

- The children fill the box with empty plastic bottles, cardboard tubes, or toys.
- They can pull the box like a wagon.
- This is great to do inside or outside.

Sockdozer

Toddlers

Socks/Pantyhose

Materials

socks
sand

To Make

- Fill a tube sock two-thirds full with sand.
- Tie the opening securely closed.

To Use

- These are great to use in the sandbox. Toddlers drag or push the "Sockdozer" through the sand to make roads.

Target Balls

Toddlers

Socks/Pantyhose

Materials
old socks
small foam balls
cardboard box

To Make
- Place a foam ball inside an old sock.
- Tie the end of the sock in a secure knot.

To Use
- Outside, the toddlers can use the cardboard box as a target to throw balls into.
- Toddlers can also just throw the balls around.

Pantyhose Balls

Toddlers

Socks/Pantyhose

Materials
pantyhose
scissors (adults only)
fiberfill

To Make
- Cut a few pairs of pantyhose into 12" lengths.
- Tie a knot in one open end of the hose and turn it inside out, so that the knot is on the inside.
- Fill the hose with fiberfill and shape it into a ball.
- Tie a knot to close the opening.

To Use

- Bring these soft balls outside so the children can throw them.
- These balls are easy to wash and dry, and safe for all ages of children.

Paper Bag Balls

 Infants/Toddlers

Bags

Materials

paper bags
newspapers
tape

To Make

- Stuff paper bags with crumpled newspapers, shaping the bags into ball shapes.
- Tape the openings closed securely.

To Use

- Infants or toddlers throw or move the lightweight balls inside or outside.

Box Tunnels

 Infants/Toddlers

 Boxes

Materials

large cardboard boxes
craft knife (adults only)
packing tape

To Make

- Away from the children, use a craft knife to remove two sides from large cardboard boxes to create simple tunnels.
- Remove any staples and cover any rough edges with tape.
- To make longer tunnels or to make tunnels with several openings, use packing tape to connect the boxes together.

To Use

- Children need no encouragement to enjoy exploring the tunnels on the playground or inside.
- Narrate the children's actions.

Garden Glove Windsocks

 Infants/Toddlers

 Gloves/Mittens

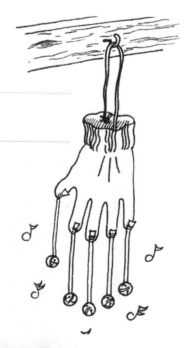

Materials

needle and thread (adults only)
jingle bells
ribbons
glue
cotton gardening gloves
short length of twine

To Make

- Thread jingle bells onto the ends of ribbons and tie them securely in place.
- Securely glue or sew ribbons onto the fingertips of a glove (see illustration).
- Then securely glue or sew both ends of a piece of twine to each side of the inside cuff of the glove to form a hanging loop.
- Hang these windsocks where breezes will make them move and jingle.

To Use

- Talk with the children about the sounds and movement of the windsocks.

Garden Glove Turtle Puppet

 Infants/Toddlers

 Gloves/Mittens

Materials

green and brown felt
scissors (adults only)
craft glue
needle and thread (adults only)
brown jersey glove
cotton balls
permanent markers (adults only)

To Make

- Cut out an oval shape from a piece of green felt.
- Glue and sew the oval onto the back of the glove. This will be the turtle's shell.
- Cut out small "spots" from brown felt.
- Glue and sew the spots on top of the green shell.
- Stuff one or two cotton balls into the middle finger of the glove to make the turtle's head.
- Draw eyes and mouth on the turtle's head.

green felt

stuff middle finger with two cotton balls.

To Use

- Place your hand inside the glove to form the puppet's head and legs.
- Use the puppet to tell stories and to interact with children as they play.
- For a variation, bring a puppet theater outside or construct a simple puppet theater using a large cardboard box with a hole cut out of the side.

Dear Parents,

We need your help to create wonderful toys for the children. Please send any of the materials that are checked. All materials should be thoroughly clean and dry.

Thank you!

- ☐ Aluminum foil or wax paper boxes
- ☐ Baskets
- ☐ Beads
- ☐ Binder clips
- ☐ Blocks
- ☐ Bubble wrap
- ☐ Butcher paper
- ☐ Cardboard boxes
- ☐ Cardboard tubes
- ☐ Catalogs
- ☐ Cellophane paper
- ☐ Cigar boxes
- ☐ Clay
- ☐ Coffee cans
- ☐ Colored chalk
- ☐ Construction paper
- ☐ Contact paper, clear or patterned
- ☐ Cookie cutters
- ☐ Cotton gloves
- ☐ Craft sticks
- ☐ Crayons
- ☐ Crepe paper streamers
- ☐ Duct tape
- ☐ Fabric
- ☐ Fabric glue
- ☐ Fabric paint
- ☐ Felt
- ☐ Gardening gloves

- ☐ Glitter
- ☐ Gloves, all sizes
- ☐ Glue
- ☐ Hair gel
- ☐ Ink pad
- ☐ Jar and juice can lids
- ☐ Jingle bells
- ☐ Lace
- ☐ Large matchboxes (sliding type)
- ☐ Magazines
- ☐ Marbles
- ☐ Markers
- ☐ Masking tape
- ☐ Mesh produce bags
- ☐ Mittens, all sizes
- ☐ Newspaper
- ☐ Oatmeal containers
- ☐ Paint
- ☐ Paintbrushes
- ☐ Pantyhose
- ☐ Paper
- ☐ Paper bags
- ☐ Paper cups
- ☐ Paper plates
- ☐ Pie tins
- ☐ Ping-Pong balls

- ☐ Pint-size milk cartons
- ☐ Pipe cleaners
- ☐ Plastic bags
- ☐ Plastic bottles and jars
- ☐ Playdough
- ☐ Popsicle sticks
- ☐ Potato chip cans
- ☐ Ribbon
- ☐ Sequins
- ☐ Sponges
- ☐ Spray bottles
- ☐ Staplers
- ☐ Straws
- ☐ Tablecloths
- ☐ Tempera paint
- ☐ Tennis balls
- ☐ Tissue boxes
- ☐ Tissue paper
- ☐ Tongue depressors
- ☐ Tube socks, all sizes
- ☐ Tweezers
- ☐ Twine
- ☐ Velcro
- ☐ Watercolors
- ☐ Wiggle eyes
- ☐ Wrapping paper
- ☐ Yarn

*Publisher permits unlimited photocopying for personal use.

Index

Available at your favorite bookstore, school supply store, or order from
Gryphon House at 800.638.0928 or www.gryphonhouse.com.

The Making Toys series...

Making Toys for Preschool Children

Using Ordinary Stuff for Extraordinary Play

Linda G. Miller and Mary Jo Gibbs

ISBN 0-87659-275-2 / Gryphon House / 18435 / PB

Making Toys for School-Age Children

Using Ordinary Stuff for Extraordinary Play

Linda G. Miller and Mary Jo Gibbs

ISBN 0-87659-276-0 / Gryphon House / 16243 / PB

This series is a teacher's dream! You'll find more creative ways to use tube socks, milk carton, and other inexpensive things found around the house than you ever imagined. Create unique, exciting toys and props to help children learn in appropriate ways. Don't recycle that cereal box...reuse it to make a simple puzzle! Each age-appropriate *Making Toys* book will make you look at everyday items in a whole new way. 2002.

First Art
Art Experiences for Toddlers and Twos

MaryAnn F. Kohl

Jump right in—doing art with toddlers and twos is fun, rewarding, and a wonderful learning experience. Children discover their world as they explore the 75 fun-filled art adventures in *First Art*. They will joyfully squeeze a rainbow, make their own (safe) beads to string, and create their very own painted paper quilt. *First Art* starts children on a journey full of exploration and creativity! 160 pages. 2002.

ISBN 0-87659-222-1 / Gryphon House / 18543 / PB

Story S-t-r-e-t-c-h-e-r-s for Infants, Toddlers, and Twos
Experiences, Activities, and Games for Popular Children's Books

Shirley Raines, Karen Miller, Leah Curry-Rood

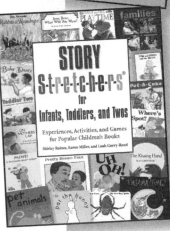

It's never too early to read to a child, especially when you have *Story S-t-r-e-t-c-h-e-r-s!* The youngest children love the repetition of words and experiences that stories provide. *Story S-t-r-e-t-c-h-e-r-s* contains suggestions for over 100 age-appropriate children's books and 240 ways to s-t-r-e-t-c-h the stories in new ways to enhance the learning process. Organized by age, this book is a wonderful addition to the *Story S-t-r-e-t-c-h-e-r-s* series, offering new ways for young children to experience the magic of a good book. Children reap amazing benefits from being exposed to reading at an early age, and *Story S-t-r-e-t-c-h-e-r-s* makes reading with infants, toddlers, and twos an adventure in learning and fun! 240 pages. 2002.

ISBN 0-87659-274-4 / Gryphon House / 18931/ PB

Games to Play with Babies-3rd Edition

Jackie Silberg

Hundreds of games to play with your baby to encourage
bonding, coordination, motor skills, and more!
At last…the eagerly awaited new edition of one of the
most trusted and popular books on infant development is
here! Completely redesigned, with 50 brand-new games
and all new illustrations, this indispensable book shows
you how to build important developmental skills while
enjoying time with your baby. Use these everyday activities
to nurture and stimulate self-confidence, coordination,
social skills, and much, much more. Give your baby a great
start with this wonderful collection of over 225 fun-filled
games! 256 pages. 2001.

ISBN 0-87659-255-8 / Gryphon House / 16285 / PB

Games to Play with Toddlers, Revised

Jackie Silberg

Revised and updated with all new illustrations and over 200
games, this indispensable book helps you develop areas
important for the growth of your 12- to 24-month-old—
areas such as language, creativity, coordination, confidence,
problem-solving, and gross motor skills. You and your
toddler will experience the joy of discovery on every fun-
filled page! 256 pages. 2002.

ISBN 0-87659-234-5 / Gryphon House / 19587 / PB

Games to Play with Two Year Olds, Revised

Jackie Silberg

Revised and updated, *Games to Play with Two Year Olds* is
packed with opportunities to build confidence and to enhance
language, coordination, social interactions, and problem-
solving skills. *Games to Play with Two Year Olds* is a must-have
for anyone caring for a child between the ages of two and three.
Turn ordinary, everyday routines into fun learning experiences!
256 pages. 2002.

ISBN 0-87659-235-3 / Gryphon House / 12687 / PB

125 Brain Games for Babies

Simple Games to Promote Early Brain Development

Jackie Silberg

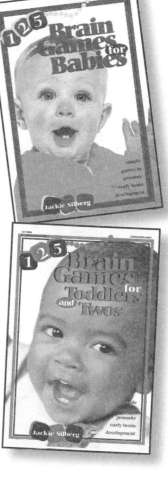

125 Brain Games for Babies is filled with enjoyable ways to build the foundation for your baby's future. There are opportunities every day to contribute to the brain development of children from birth through twelve months. Each game has an annotation on the latest brain research, and a discussion of the ways it will develop brain power in your baby. These simple games create the brain connections needed for future learning while you are having fun! 160 pages. 1999.

ISBN 0-87659-199-3 / Gryphon House 19854 / PB

125 Brain Games for Toddlers and Twos

Simple Games to Promote Early Brain Development

Jackie Silberg

A young child's brain grows at a phenomenal rate in the first years of life, opening a window of opportunity for learning that occurs only once in a lifetime. *125 Brain Games for Toddlers and Twos* is a fun-filled collection of ways to lay the groundwork for your child's future. It is packed with everyday opportunities to contribute to brain development during the critical period from 12-36 months. 160 pages. 2000.

ISBN 0-87659-205-1 / Gryphon House / 13984 / PB

• Early Childhood News Director's Award

THE INNOVATIONS CURRICULUM

Kay Albrecht and Linda G. Miller

Everything you need for a complete infant and toddler
program. The *Innovations* curriculum series is a
comprehensive, interactive curriculum for infants and
toddlers. Responding to children's interests is at the
heart of emergent curriculum and central to the
Innovations series, which meets a full spectrum of needs
for teachers, parents, and the children they care for. In
addition to the wealth of activities, each book includes
these critical components:

- Applying child development theory to everyday
  experiences
- Using assessment to meet individual developmental
  needs of infants and toddlers
- Using the physical environment as a learning tool
- Developing a partner relationship with parents
- Fostering an interactive climate in the classroom
- Educating parents

The *Innovations* series is a unique combination of the
practical and theoretical. It combines them in a way that
provides support for beginning teachers, information for
experienced teachers, and a complete program for every
teacher!

Innovations: The Comprehensive Infant Curriculum

496 pages. 2000.

ISBN 0-87659-213-2 / Gryphon House / 14962 / PB

- Early Childhood News Director's Award

Innovations: The Comprehensive Toddler Curriculum

608 pages. 2000.

ISBN 0-87659-214-0 / Gryphon House / 17846 / PB

- Early Childhood News Director's Award

Innovations: Infant and Toddler Development

Kay Albrecht and Linda G. Miller
This comprehensive resource provides teachers with a thorough understanding of the knowledge base that informs early childhood practice. Focusing on the development of children from birth to age three, *Innovations* gives you an in-depth guide to the underlying ages and stages, theories, and best practices of the early childhood field, so you can create opportunities for infants and toddlers to learn and teachers to teach.

Enhance interactions and classroom environment with wide-ranging understanding of infant and toddler development. Topics include:
- managing normal aggression
- theories of infant and toddler development
- best practices
- the development of language skills
- teaching social problem-solving
- guidance and discipline. 384 pages. 2001.

ISBN 0-87659-259-0 / Gryphon House / 19237 / PB

Innovations: The Comprehensive Infant and Toddler Curriculum

Trainer's Guide
ISBN 0-87659-260-4 / Gryphon House / 15826 / PB

Innovations: The Comprehensive Infant Curriculum

A Self-Directed Teacher's Guide
ISBN 0-87659-270-1 / Gryphon House / 15384 / PB

Innovations: The Comprehensive Toddler Curriculum

A Self-Directed Teacher's Guide
ISBN 0-87659-233-7 / Gryphon House / 16571 / PB

Simple Steps

Developmental Activities for Infants, Toddlers, and Two-Year-Olds

Karen Miller

Open the door to teaching infants, toddlers, and
two-year-olds successfully with these 300 activities
linked to the recent research in child development.
Simple Steps outlines a typical developmental
sequence in ten areas: social/emotional, fine motor,
gross motor, language, cognitive, sensory, nature,
music and movement, creativity, and dramatic play.
296 pages. 1999.

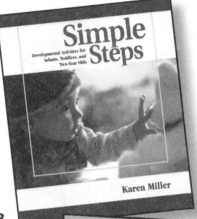

ISBN 0-87659-204-3 / Gryphon House / 18274 / PB

Go Anywhere Games for Babies

Jackie Silberg

Have you ever needed just a little help when you were out
with your baby? More than 60 fun games designed to play
on the bus, in the waiting room, at the park, or right at
home. Written by the best-selling baby game author Jackie
Silberg, it's printed on extra-heavy coated paper for
maximum durability, and uses a special binding that lies
flat on any surface—even a parent's knee! Sections include
games for babies birth to 3 months, 3-6 months, 6-9 months
and 9-12 months, plus a bonus section of going-to-sleep games.
84 pages. 2000.

ISBN 1-58904-006-6 / Robins Lane Press /16925 / Wiro Spine

• Early Childhood News Director's Award

Available at your favorite bookstore, school supply store, or order from
Gryphon House at 800.638.0928 or www.gryphonhouse.com.

Toddlers Together

The Complete Planning Guide for a Toddler Curriculum

Cynthia Catlin

Children one to three years old experience the joy of learning all year long with these hands-on, seasonal activities. *Toddlers Together* brings you fun, easy-to-do activities geared toward the toddler's unique stage of development. 319 pages. 1994.

ISBN 0-87659-171-3 / Gryphon House / 17721 / PB

More Toddlers Together

The Complete Planning Guide for a Toddler Curriculum, Vol. II

Cynthia Catlin

More Toddlers Together is arranged seasonally and packed with over 200 activities organized by theme within each season. Additions include 19 new themes, how to set up learning centers for toddlers, suggestions of toys, books, and materials to use with toddlers, a suggested daily schedule, and a sample newsletter. This is a complete curriculum resource for teachers of toddlers. 272 pages. 1996.

ISBN 0-87659-179-9 / Gryphon House / 16509 / PB